Money
and
the Economy
A Monetarist View

William Poole
Brown University

▲▲
ADDISON-WESLEY PUBLISHING COMPANY

Reading, Massachusetts • Menlo Park, California
London • Amsterdam • Don Mills, Ontario • Sydney

PERSPECTIVES ON ECONOMICS SERIES

Michael L. Wachter & Susan M. Wachter, Editors

PUBLISHED

**Development, The International Economic Order
and Commodity Agreements,** *Jere R. Behrman*
**The Economics of Medical Care:
A Policy Perspective,** *Joseph P. Newhouse*
Money and Economy: A Monetarist View, *William Poole*
Antitrust Policies and Issues, *Roger Sherman*
Income Distribution and Redistribution, *Paul J. Taubman*

AVAILABLE IN LATE 1978 AND EARLY 1979

Labor Unions, *George H. Hildebrand*
Forecasting, *Lawrence R. Klein & Richard M. Young*
International Trade, *Stephen P. Magee*
Regulation, *Roger G. Noll*
Population, *T. Paul Schultz*
Urban Economics, *Susan M. Wachter*

ISBN 0-201-08364-7
BCDEFGHIJK-AL-798

To
Grandmother Poole,
whose continuing curiosity about the
world around her proves that age need
not lead to assumed answers replacing
new questions.

Foreword

The PERSPECTIVES ON ECONOMICS series has been developed to present economics students with up-to-date policy-oriented books written by leading scholars in this field. Many professors and students have stressed the need for flexible, contemporary materials that provide an understanding of current policy issues.

In general, beginning students in economics are not exposed to the controversial material and development of current issues that are the basis of research in economics. Because of their length and breadth of coverage, textbooks tend to lack current economic thinking on policy questions; in attempting to provide a balanced viewpoint, they often do not give the reader a feel for the lively controversy in each field. With this series, we have attempted to fill this void.

The books in this series are designed to complement standard text-books. Each volume reflects the research interests and views of the authors. Thus these books can also serve as basic reading material in the specific topic courses covered by each. The stress throughout is on the careful development of institutional factors and policy in the context of economic theory. Yet the exposition is designed to be accessible to undergraduate students and interested laypersons with an elementary background in economics.

Michael L. Wachter
Susan M. Wachter

Preface

When Michael Wachter called me about this project I accepted readily. For some time I have felt that a book bringing together monetarist theory, evidence, and policy views at a relatively elementary level was needed. Not only in the classroom but also around the lunch table at the faculty club I have found pervasive ignorance about the most elementary monetary relationships. I have often wished I could pull out of my pocket a simple chart showing the relationship between money and prices, or money growth and the business cycle, as I struggled to make myself understood.

In a sense, *Money and the Economy* represents an attempt to provide a few simple charts and some accompanying text. My aim has been to explain the first-order monetary effects on important magnitudes and to explain the major policy issues. I have also tried to develop the reader's understanding of the nature and origins of common mistakes of monetary analysis. And I have attempted to provide a feeling for which propositions should be regarded as more, and which as less, well established.

I have made no attempt to characterize the thought of any particular major contributor to what has come to be known as "monetarism," or to attribute particular propositions to particular writers; however, my intellectual debts will probably be clear enough to the monetary economist. The book has been written as a treatise for the instructory student—not, of course, a treatise in the sense of a work presenting new findings but rather in the sense of presenting my views on the major issues in monetarism. No effort has been made to pursue the textbook approach of presenting in neutral fashion all sides of controversial issues; a book on monetarism ought to be quite clear about what at least one monetarist believes.

The next-to-last draft of the book was read very carefully by Michael Wachter and by two anonymous referees. Their detailed comments were extremely helpful in preparing the final draft, and I thank them. I also want to thank the typists at the Federal Reserve Bank of San Franciso, where I spent the summer of 1977 as Visiting Scholar, for typing during the day the material I wrote the previous evening; and Sally Deslauriers, Carol Massey, and Marion Wathey, all of Brown University, who typed the final draft under great time pressure in December, 1977.

Finally, and certainly not least, I thank my wife, Mary Lynne, for putting up with me all those evenings and "one last" Saturdays when I neglected her to work on the book.

January 1978   W.P.

Contents

INTRODUCTION   1

Suggestion for Further Reading   4

MONEY AND PRICES I   5

Some Evidence   6
    The United States Experience   8
    Hyperinflation   11
Interpreting the Evidence   11
The Quantity Theory of Money   17
    The Equation of Exchange   17
    The Cambridge k 20
Summary   22
References   22
Suggestions for Further Reading   23

MONEY AND PRICES II   24

Methods of Money Creation and Their Price Level Effects   25
    Currency Reform Money   25
    Helicopter Money   26
    Deficit Money   33
    Open-Market Money   37
    Methods of Money Creation: Summary   37
Inflationary Equilibrium   38
    Self-Generating Inflations   40
Summary   40

MONEY AND OUTPUT   42

The Problem of Causation   45
The Monetary Theory of the Business Cycle   47
    The Demand for Money   47
    Effects of a Monetary Contraction   49
    Short-Run Price Adjustment   52
The Theory Restated   54
Stagflation   55
Nonmonetary Causes of Business Fluctuations   59
    Shifts in the Demand for Money   59
    Shifts in the Demand for Goods   60
    Price Disturbances   61
Money and Output in the Long Run   62
Summary   63
Reference   64
Suggestions for Further Reading   64

MONEY AND INTEREST RATES   65

The Simple Arithmetic of Interest   65
The Four Types of Loans   67
Real versus Nominal Interest Rates   69
The Effects of Inflation on Interest Rates   70
The Business Cycle Pattern of Interest Rates   74
Summary of Monetary Effects on Interest Rates   76
Reference   76

THE CREATION AND DESTRUCTION OF MONEY   77

Commercial Banks   77
The Central Bank   84
The United States Treasury   88
The Monetary Base   90
Summary   92
Suggestion for Further Reading   93

MONETARY POLICY   94

Scientific Issues   94
Short-Run Stabilization Policy   97
Relationship of Monetary to Fiscal Policy   99
Historical Evaluation of Monetary Policy   103
The Role of Interest Rates in Monetary Policy   105

Reasons for Monetary Instability   106
    Financing War   107
    Interest Rate Smoothing   107
    Reducing Balance-of-Payments Deficits   108
    Stabilizing Thrift Institutions and Housing Construction   108
    Evaluating the Arguments   108
Federal Reserve Preferences   111
Monetary Policy Rules versus Discretion   111
Summary   114
Suggestions for Further Reading   115

INDEX   116

Introduction 1

What is monetarism? "Monetarism," like other "ism" words, misleads almost as much as it describes. One definition of monetarism states that it is the set of propositions that monetarists believe. But two monetarists in a room, like any other two economists, are certain to have at least three views on any subject!

While no simple set of propositions can be said to define monetarism, the term is not entirely empty. Suppose several dozen economists who think of themselves as monetarists—rather than as Keynesians, nonmonetarists, or fiscalists—were asked to write down five or ten key propositions about the effects of monetary changes and recommendations for monetary policy. Of the total number of propositions produced by the group of monetarist economists, we might find that any particular member of the group would subscribe to 70 percent, while any particular Keynesian might subscribe to only 30 percent. A similar exercise with Keynesian propositions might find any particular Keynesian supporting 70 percent and any particular monetarist supporting only 30 percent.

In an attempt to capture the basic flavor of monetarism the following eight propositions are offered:

1. Inflation is a monetary phenomenon. A 10-percent change in the quantity of money will produce a 10-percent change in the price level, although probably not immediately.
2. In the short run, while the price adjustment process is working itself out, a change in the rate of growth of money, especially if it is unanticipated, will affect the level of national output. Indeed, the business cycle—boom and recession—is primarily caused by monetary instability.
3. The long-run trend rate of growth of a nation's output is completely independent, or almost so, of the level and rate of growth of the nation's money stock.

4. The level of nominal interest rates depends importantly on the rate of inflation and, therefore, on the rate of growth of the money stock.
5. The high correlations that exist between the money stock and a number of other variables reflect a line of causation running from the money stock to the other variables and not the other way around.
6. It is technically feasible to control the money stock and, therefore, the government should be held responsible for the consequences of monetary instability.
7. The attempt to use deliberate changes in the money stock to offset disturbances originating in the private sector has been a failure; the monetary authorities ought simply to maintain a constant rate of growth of the money stock.
8. In analyzing why the world works as it does, it is best to accept the premise that households and firms are rational utility- and profit-maximizers.

Although different economists will no doubt quarrel with the precise statement of these propositions, most will feel that the propositions do capture the flavor of monetarism and will probably agree that it is futile to attempt to *define* monetarism. Some, however, may question especially the inclusion of the eighth proposition.

The eighth proposition reflects the fact that nonmonetarist theories of money, prices, business cycles, and interest rates tend to rely on nonprofit maximizing assumptions. Prices are frequently assumed to be rigid, sticky, or institutionally determined. Economic agents are frequently assumed to be poorly informed about matters on which more complete information is available.

Monetarist analysis does not, of course, deny the existence of institutions, but insists that institutions are shaped importantly by economic forces. The effect of money growth on inflation, for example, will depend on the nature of a nation's institutions *in the short run,* but in the long run the institutions themselves will change in response to inflation. Understanding institutional processes, therefore, is not fundamental to understanding inflation because these processes are only an interesting sideshow.

Keynesian proponents of activist monetary and fiscal policies to stabilize the economy frequently argue, implicitly or explicitly, that government policymakers can be better informed than representative households and firms. Monetarists, on the other hand, are usually skeptical of this claim. Information provides opportunity for profit, and profits are not ordinarily ignored in the private sector. Much of the basis for successful activist government stabilization policy disappears if policymakers are no better informed than representative market-makers are. Both will make mistakes, and so government policy designed to offset what are thought to be private mistakes will itself be as often mistaken as correct. The typical monetarist position opposing activist stabilization policies probably depends as much on the eighth proposition as it does on the observation that stabilization policy has not in fact been very effective in the past.

All the chapters except the last are meant to be concerned with scientific propositions only—propositions about the effects of money without regard to the normative issues of whether those effects are good or bad or how money *ought* to be controlled. Nevertheless, it is very difficult to discuss certain scientific issues without using loaded words. How can an inflation of 1000 percent *per month* be discussed without at least hinting that the event is unfortunate, and therefore implicitly discussing the policy issue of whether the money creation causing the inflation is or is not desirable? Moreover, any use of graphic words in an effort to make the presentation more readable inevitably injects loaded words into what in principle should be a dispassionate scientific analysis of what causes what. In spite of the sometimes colorful words used, conclusions on policy issues should be delayed, since policy analysis involves questions of trading off one good thing for another, or one bad thing for another. All the "anothers" must be presented before trade-off issues are analyzed.

Monetary policy itself is discussed in the last chapter. Even here, however, practically no attention is paid to the normative issues concerning the relative merits of different policy effects; for example, the question of whether it is worth accepting more inflation to attain lower unemployment is not examined. The reason that issues of this type are ignored is that disputes over monetary policy are almost entirely disputes over scientific issues—over whether a particular policy will in fact produce the advertised results. It is hoped that the monetary policy chapter will clarify this issue as well as explain why monetary authorities continue to make the same mistakes time and time again.

The scientific chapters explain the effects of monetary changes on inflation (Chapters 2 and 3), on employment (Chapter 4), and on interest rates (Chapter 5). An effort is made to explain not only *what* happens but *why* it happens. Also important at many points in the discussion is an explanation of "why nots?"—of why a particular event such as inflation is necessarily a monetary phenomenon and not the result of some other cause.

Chapter 6, "The Creation and Destruction of Money," is to some extent peripheral and may be skipped by anyone convinced that the government can control the stock of money and can, therefore, be held responsible for any changes in it. But this issue is often hotly debated between monetarists and nonmonetarists. The merits of the policy prescription for a steady rate of money growth are sometimes not seriously discussed because the question of the *feasibility* of money stock control dominates debate. The basic mechanics of money creation and destruction are discussed in Chapter 6 to show that any questions about feasibility are not questions economic analysis can answer; rather they are questions concerning the political willingness of a government to control money creation.

SUGGESTION FOR FURTHER READING

Mayer, Thomas, 1975. The structure of monetarism, I and II. *Kredit and Kapital* 3, 4: 191-218, 293-316.

Money 2
and
Prices I

In November of 1923 the price level in Germany was over one *billion* times its level 16 months earlier, and the amount of German money in circulation had increased almost as much. For some Germans the disaster was complete; hardworking, prosperous, and thrifty families were reduced to a state of poverty. Others, better able to guess the twists and turns of wildly accelerating prices, had become rich. Ever since its occurrence, this dramatic inflationary episode has intrigued economists and laymen alike. As anyone who has lived through a hyperinflation will attest, an understanding of the theory of inflation is of more than academic interest.

If economics courses were organized as courses in psychology and medicine are, the study of hyper- (extreme, or runaway) inflation would appear in a course on economic pathology. Although relatively moderate inflations (up to, perhaps, several hundred percent per year) may continue for many years, hyperinflation produces such disorder that the currency always "dies." The money becomes worthless; a foreign currency begins to circulate in place of the local currency, or the government introduces a new currency as one part of a currency reform package including provisions designed to end explosive money growth.

The disorder of an economy during a period of hyperinflation is a fascinating topic of study in its own right. But more important for the purposes of this book, it is an instructive topic of study because cause and effect relationships, hidden by a host of other factors during mild inflations, stand out clearly during hyperinflation. Foreign episodes of hyperinflation are directly relevant to understanding the United States experience not because there is any substantial danger at the present time, or in the foreseeable future, that mild inflation in the United States could turn into hyperinflation, but because these episodes are the closest things to controlled

5

monetary experiments economists have to observe. Big causes, by swamping all other factors in importance, effectively control for a host of other factors that economists—who must rely on natural rather than carefully designed, controlled experiments—know may in principle be important.

Unlike many pathological cases in psychology and medicine, the cause of hyperinflation is fully understood: every known case has been caused by enormous increases in the amount of money in circulation. Moreover, in no case has it been observed that huge increases in the amount of money have failed to cause hyperinflation. Similarly, although it is necessary to consider the importance of nonmonetary factors, increases in the money stock have been by far the most important single factor causing inflationary episodes in the United States.

While it is frequently difficult to know what caused, or permitted, any particular monetary expansion, knowledge that a monetary expansion is the proximate cause of inflation—the factor in a causal chain closest to the inflation itself—is of great importance. A proposed remedy that does not stop excessive monetary expansion will not be successful in stopping inflation, while any remedy, no matter how peculiar, that does end the excessive monetary expansion will end the inflation. The purpose of this chapter and the following one is to explain why this statement is true.

Two features of inflation require a solid theoretical understanding. First, increases in the average price level are closely related to increases in the money stock. Second, in spite of enormous increases in the amount of money in circulation, people living through hyperinflation typically find that there is a *scarcity* of money compared with the amount of their everyday spending. This apparent paradox has a ready explanation, as shown below, but failure to resolve the paradox has frequently aggravated inflation; under great pressure to stop a hyperinflation, public officials, and economists, have frequently argued that the inflation was not being caused by excessive money issue and, further, that apparent money scarcities *required* further money issues. The same principles apply to mild inflations, but the milder the inflation, the milder the effects.

To explain the basic economic theory involved, this chapter and the next are devoted to the two fundamental points outlined above. As good a starting point as any is to "take a look at the facts."

SOME EVIDENCE

Theory, especially economic theory, is frequently dull and tedious until it is realized that the theory really does produce order out of a chaos of facts, and really does provide explanations for puzzling and disturbing phenomena. It seems best, therefore, to begin the analysis not with some theory but with some facts: the historical facts of prices and money in the United States and the dramatic facts of several foreign episodes of hyperinflation.

The reader should understand, however, that these facts, like most facts, are not simply thrown up by nature to float around awaiting a theory to explain them. Few facts exist without a theory: at a simple level, for example, the money stock facts for the United States described below would not be available were it not for the efforts of the economists who collected the data *because* the money stock facts were of central importance in testing a theory. And at a deeper level, the processing of raw data from old bank records and other sources into something called "money stock data" could not have occurred without the theoretical construct "money."

Accompanying the presentation of the facts, therefore, is a discussion explaining the elementary theory of the relationships between money and prices. Following this discussion of evidence, the elementary theory will be restated more precisely and the finer points then discussed in the next chapter. But, for now, just what are the "facts"?

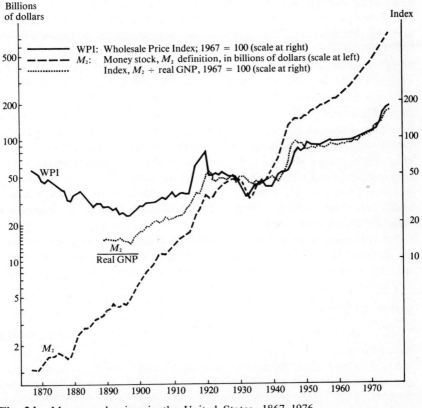

Fig. 2.1   Money and prices in the United States, 1867–1976.

The United States Experience

The solid and dashed lines in Fig. 2.1 show money and prices for the United States for the 110-year period from 1867 to 1976. (The dotted line in the figure will be discussed later.) This period was selected because 1867 is the first year for which reasonably reliable annual data on the United States money stock are available, and because 1976 is the last full year at the time of this writing. Close inspection of this figure will be rewarding.

The figure has been drawn using a logarithmic, or ratio, scale on the vertical axis. The logarithmic scale has the property that equal distances on the scale represent equal *percentage* differences. Thus, the change in the money stock from about $20 billion in 1880 to about $40 billion in 1890 requires the same vertical distance in the figure as does the change in the money stock from about $100 billion in 1944 to $200 billion in 1958. The use of the logarithmic scale reflects the fact that for the data being examined the significance of changes depends on their percentage magnitudes. For example, to be told that a price has increased by five dollars tells the buyer little without knowledge of whether the product's price used to be $10, or $100, or $1000, or whatever. Similarly, a $100 increase in my bank account is much more significant to *me* than is a $100 increase in a millionaire's bank account to *him or her*, and much less significant to *me* than was a $100 increase in my father's bank account to *him* in the middle of the Great Depression.

Over the entire period shown in Fig. 2.1 it is clear that the money stock has risen much more rapidly than the level of prices. Indeed, from 1867 to 1895 prices were generally falling. Nevertheless, close examination of the figure suggests that periods with higher rates of growth of the money stock have generally been associated with higher rates of increase (or slower rates of decrease) of the price level. Particularly noteworthy are wartime periods and periods immediately after wars. Major and minor wars occurred 1897–1898 (Spanish American War), 1914–1919 (World War I), 1939–1945 (World War II), 1950–1953 (Korean War), and 1965–1972 (Vietnam War).[1] If a longer period had been shown (the United States Wholesale Price Index is available on an annual basis back to 1749), then the importance of wars would have been even clearer; major inflations accompanied the Revolutionary War, the War of 1812, and the Civil War as well as the wars after 1867.

One explanation of why prices have typically risen during and just after wars is that military expenditures add to the total demand for goods and services, and divert production from civilian uses. This explanation is not

---

[1] The dates used reflect United States involvement, either of a direct military nature or as a supplier to combatant nations, significant enough to affect the United States economy. Some may dispute the exact dates selected, but for the purpose at hand precise dating is unimportant.

necessarily inconsistent with the monetary explanation provided that an explanation of the wartime increases in the money stock is provided, a matter taken up in Chapter 7. In this chapter and the next the questions will be: (1) could these inflations have occurred without the increases in the money stock? and (2) could these inflations have been avoided given that the money stock increased?

It was noted earlier that the United States money stock grew much more rapidly over the period covered by Fig. 2.1 than did the United States price level. Indeed, in the figure the relationship between money and prices seems so loose that few would, from this evidence, feel that the level of the nation's money stock had much to do with the level of prices. However, most of the difference between the growth in the price level and the growth in the money stock is explained by the fact that the United States economy grew substantially over this period.

To understand this point, consider a simple example concerning a 19th-century farmer and a blacksmith who makes and repairs the farmer's tools and farm implements. The farmer grows food, eats some of it, and sells the rest at the town market. The income he receives may be partly saved, but most is spent on a variety of things, including purchases from the blacksmith. Similarly, the blacksmith may save some of the income he receives, but most is spent on a variety of things, including purchases of food at the town market. Suppose that there is a constant fixed amount of money in existence—X dollars per capita—and that it circulates from farmer to blacksmith and back again. Of course, there would be no need for money if the economy consisted of *only* one farmer and one blacksmith; money is important precisely because there are lots of farmers, blacksmiths, shoemakers, tinkers, candlemakers, fishermen, patent medicine peddlers, and economists all doing business with each other.

Now suppose new immigrants come to the United States, and become farmers and blacksmiths. More food is produced, and more tools and farm implements. If more money is somehow produced, and the amount of new money equals X dollars for each of the new immigrants, then the simple economy described above can function as before except that the size of the population, the total amount of food produced each year, and the amount of money in circulation have all grown in the *same* proportion.

But suppose the amount of money in circulation does not grow as immigrants arrive. Then what? The key to this question is that ten dollars will do as much "work" when the price of wheat is one dollar a bushel as will eight dollars when the price of wheat is 80 cents per bushel. In each case the amount of wheat that can be purchased is ten bushels. Thus, if the quantity of money in circulation does not increase when the population increases, that fixed number of dollars—a smaller number of dollars *per capita*—can do more work if the prices of wheat and other goods fall.

If the number of dollars in circulation increases in proportion to the population, then no decrease in the prices of goods is necessary. Clearly, the larger amount of "money work" to be done with a larger population can be managed if each dollar does more work by having lower prices, or if the number of dollars increases while prices remain the same, or some combination.

A few numbers illustrate how this argument can be applied to the United States experience as shown in Fig. 2.1. In 1976 the United States population was about 5.8 times the United States population in 1867, but the money stock in 1976 was about 550 times the money stock in 1867. On a per capita basis, then, the money stock in 1976 was 95.5 times its level in 1867. But over this period the price level rose to 3.2 times its 1867 level. The large discrepancy between 95.5 and 3.2 can be accounted for in large measure by considering the large increase in per capita production.

To understand the importance of growth in production, let us return to the farmer–blacksmith example. It was argued that an increase in the number of farmers and blacksmiths will increase the amount of money-work to be done. Now suppose that the population is constant, but that each farmer and each blacksmith becomes more productive. The farmer, for example, may produce more food by using more land, improved plows, better seed, and so forth. Similarly, the blacksmith may produce more tools by using improved production techniques. Even though, by assumption, population has not grown in this example, production has grown and there is more to be sold at the town's markets and shops. With the larger amount of production, there is more money-work to be done as goods are bought and sold. As before, to perform this work the economy needs some combination of lower prices and more dollars in circulation.

To reflect these considerations, it is useful to measure a nation's money stock in terms of money per unit of national output. This adjustment allows for changes in both population and in output per capita. The dotted line in Fig. 2.1 shows an index of the United States money stock, using the M_2 definition (currency outstanding plus commercial bank demand and time deposits held by the general public), per unit of real output (measured as real GNP). Unfortunately, reasonably accurate annual estimates of United States output begin only in 1889 and so the dotted line does not extend back to 1867.

The relationship between money and prices can now be seen to be much closer than it first appeared. Whereas the money stock in 1976 was almost 200 times its 1889 level, the money stock per unit of real GNP in 1976 was 11.2 times the corresponding figure for 1889. Since the price index in 1976 was 6.4 times its level in 1889, it can be seen that the single, simple adjustment of allowing for growth in real GNP eliminates most of the discrepancy between the magnitudes of the money stock and price level increases since 1889. Moreover, Fig. 2.1 makes it clear that most of the discrepancy between increases in money per unit of real GNP and increases in prices occurred before 1920. The apparent change in the relationship between money per unit of real GNP and prices around 1920 may reflect the extensive changes in the economy since that time—the higher standard of living, the greatly enlarged role of the government, the regulation of interest rates on time deposits, and prohibition of interest on demand deposits starting in the 1930s, and so forth—or it may reflect improvements in the data.[2]

In spite of the impressive relationship shown in Fig. 2.1, it is clear that the money-price relationship, even after allowing for changes in production, is far from perfect. The timing of changes in money and prices is not always the same, and the relative magnitude of the changes differs from one episode to another. Some, but not all, of these features can be explained by the more refined analysis presented in Chapter 3.

Hyperinflation

The relationship between the quantity of money in circulation and the price level stands out especially clearly during hyperinflation. If the money stock increases by 1000 times over the course of a year, an adjustment for a rising level of real output is so relatively unimportant that it is not worth the bother. If, for example, the money stock is 1000 times higher while real output has risen by six percent, then money per unit of real GNP is 943 times instead of 1000 times higher. In a case such as this, it is much more productive for the researcher to spend time improving the accuracy of the money stock and price data than to investigate whether real output rose by six percent, or four percent, or whatever.

Figures 2.2–2.5 show the money stock and the price level for four different episodes of hyperinflation. These inflations differ in magnitude; in the famous German inflation in the early 1920s the price level rose by over one *billion* times (1.02×10^{10}) between August, 1922 and November, 1923— while in the Hungarian inflation in 1945–1946, the price level rose by over one *octillion* times (5.20×10^{27}) in the space of 13 months. Perhaps these numbers will be better understood if we note that the German inflation, on average, involved price level increases at a compound rate of 322 percent per *month* while the Hungarian episode involved price increases averaging 19,800 percent per *month*.[3]

INTERPRETING THE EVIDENCE

The relationship between money and prices is clearly impressively close in the hyperinflation episodes. Indeed, when examining periods of hyperinfla-

---

2 The GNP estimates are thought to be quite reliable for 1929 and later years, reasonably reliable from 1919 to 1928, and more questionable for earlier years. See *Historical Statistics of the United States*, pp. 215-223.

3 The figures reported in this paragraph are from Table 1 in Cagan 1956, p. 26.

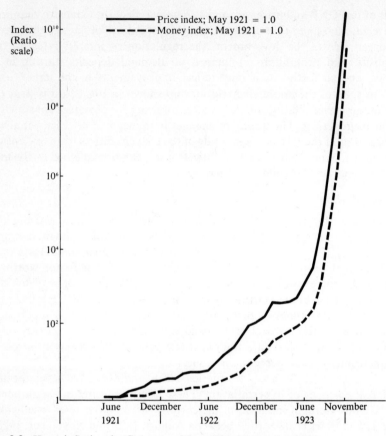

Price index; May 1921 = 1.0
Money index; May 1921 = 1.0

Fig. 2.2 Hyperinflation in Germany, May 1921–November 1923.

tion it is hard to imagine any other result. But a careful examination of Figs. 2.2–2.5 will reveal that in every case prices rose more rapidly than the money stock over the course of the inflation. Why should that be?

Consider a simple thought-experiment. Suppose the price of everything you buy were suddenly 100 times higher *and* your flow of income from wages, interest, dividends, and all other sources were also 100 times higher. That is, if you are now receiving $500 per month, in this thought-experiment you are receiving $50,000 per month, but because all prices have risen 100 times your monthly income of $50,000 buys the same amount of goods as your present income of $500.

Suppose further that your average cash holding in the thought-experiment is the *same* as it is now. That is, if your monthly income is now $500

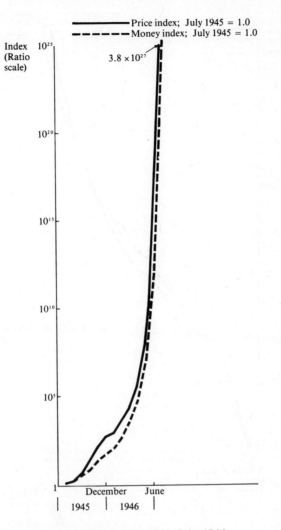

Fig. 2.3 Hyperinflation in Hungary, July 1945–July 1946.

and you hold $100 in cash—currency and coin plus bank accounts—on the average over the month, then in the thought-experiment your average cash holding is still only $100.

To be sure this thought-experiment is understood, consider your cash holding behavior a little further. Suppose your current income of $500 per month takes the form of a monthly paycheck. When you receive the pay-check you deposit it in a bank and spend the money over the month until the

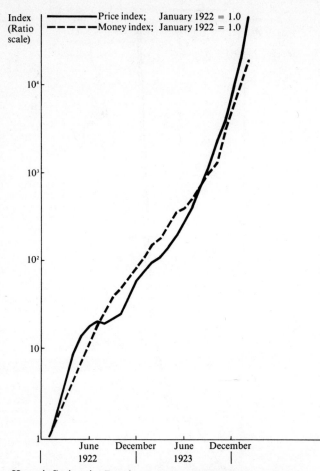

Index (Ratio scale)

———— Price index;   January 1922 = 1.0
- - - - Money index;   January 1922 = 1.0

10^4

10^3

10^2

10

1

June   December   June   December
1922   1923

Fig. 2.4 Hyperinflation in Russia, January 1922–February 1924.

checking account is about empty at the end of the month, at which time the next paycheck arrives. Your cash balance is relatively large at the beginning of the month, and relatively small at the end of the month, averaging out to $100 over the month.

If your monthly paycheck were $50,000, it would seem that everything could proceed as before if your average monthly cash balance were $10,000. But in the thought-experiment you are only allowed to have $100. "How can that be?" you may ask. "No one tells me how much cash I am allowed to hold. If I want to hold more than $100, I'll accumulate cash by not spending all of my $50,000 paycheck some month."

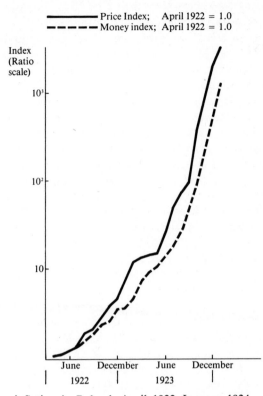

Fig. 2.5 Hyperinflation in Poland, April 1922–January 1924.

But—and here's the key point—the *total* stock of money in this experiment has not changed. If you hold more than $100, then someone else will have to hold less than before. For example, by not spending some of your paycheck, the store from which you had been buying will take in less money than before. Moreover, everyone is in the same boat. All wages, prices, incomes, and so forth, are 100 times higher, and so everyone wants to hold larger cash balances. Everyone will be trying to reduce spending for just a little while until his or her cash balance can be built up. But if everyone is trying to increase cash balances, then there is *no* possibility that everyone can succeed if the *total* amount of cash in existence is fixed.

The effects of attempts to add to cash balances are discussed more fully in Chapter 4, but note two things at this point. First, if you attempt to build up your cash by reducing spending for a time, then the stores that had been planning on your spending will find themselves with unsold goods piling up on the shelves. Similarly, if firms attempt to build up their cash balances by, say, laying off some employees for a time, then those employees will not be receiving the paychecks they had been counting on.

Second, if the price and wage increases of 100 times could somehow be rolled back enough, then life could go on as before. How much is "enough"? "Enough" is the point at which people *in general* are no longer trying to increase their cash balances.

This thought-experiment was worked out under the assumption that your paycheck was received monthly, and that with a $500 monthly paycheck you held $100 in cash on the average. But suppose you were paid weekly—four paychecks per month of $125 each. In this case your average cash balance could be lower. Instead of having to hold sufficient cash so that your $500 paycheck would last the month, now the task is to make the $125 paycheck last the week. With weekly paychecks your *monthly* income is still $500 but your average cash balance can be lower.

How much lower could your average cash balance be? While $100 average cash balance is clearly too low if your monthly paycheck is $50,000, might a $100 average cash balance suffice if your weekly paycheck were $10,250? Probably not. What about a *daily* paycheck of $2500 (assuming an average of 20 working days per month)? Or paychecks of $1250 twice a day?

Now we're getting down to reasonable numbers! If $100 average cash balance was satisfactory for a paycheck of $500, it is not unreasonable to believe that $50 average cash balance for a paycheck of $500 might be workable. All that is needed is greater resort to credit cards and similar devices, and then payment of bills when the paycheck arrives. A $50 average cash balance on a monthly paycheck of $500 is a cash balance of ten percent of the monthly paycheck. In the thought-experiment a $100 average cash balance is eight percent of the $1250 paycheck received twice a day.

Can these numbers possibly be "reasonable" as suggested at the beginning of the last paragraph? As fantastic as it seems, at the end of the great German inflation people really were being paid twice a day. Workers would spend their morning paychecks at lunchtime and their afternoon paychecks on their way home from work. Why? Inflation was proceeding at such a dizzy pace that shops had blackboards and prices were marked up hour by hour. If you weren't paid at noon for your morning's work, then the pay when received at the end of the day would buy a good deal less.

But the consequence of being paid so frequently and spending so rapidly is a *scarcity* of money. When your monthly pay was $500 and your average cash balance $100, on average your cash balance was four times your daily rate of pay of $25 (assuming 20 working days per month) and, therefore, four times the goods and services you bought on the average from the earnings of a day's labor. But in our thought-experiment your average cash balance of $100 was only 0.4 times your daily rate of pay of $2500 and, therefore, only 0.4 times the goods and services you bought from the earnings of a day's labor.

There is a scarcity of money in the sense of a scarcity of a *reserve of purchasing power over goods.* But the scarcity of purchasing power comes about precisely because the excessive growth in the quantity of money forces prices up so rapidly that it is too expensive for individuals to hold a reserve of purchasing power in the form of money, and they do not do so. Excessive growth in the *nominal* quantity of money produces a scarcity in the *real* quantity of money—the nominal quantity of money adjusted for prices. In a hyperinflation, the only way to end the scarcity of money is to stop printing so much.

It is no doubt true that the same tendency for the real quantity of money to decline in an inflation exists in the United States, but United States inflations have never been large enough for this tendency to appear unambiguously in the data. A rate of inflation of ten percent or more per *year* is very rare in United States history; in contrast, of the four hyperinflations shown in Figs. 2.2–2.5 the Russian inflation proceeded at the slowest average rate—57 percent per *month.*

THE QUANTITY THEORY OF MONEY

The preceding discussion has presented what is usually called the quantity theory of money, but what might better be called the quantity of money theory of the price level. Two different formalizations of the theory—the equation of exchange and the Cambridge *k*—help to provide a deeper insight into the economic processes connecting money and prices. The two formalizations were developed at about the same time, late in the 19th and early in the 20th century (although the basic quantity theory idea is much older). The clearest statement of the equation of exchange approach was by the great American economist Irving Fisher, while the Cambridge *k* approach was derived by a group of economists, of whom Alfred Marshall was the most important, at Cambridge University in England.

The Equation of Exchange

The equation of exchange is an identity derived from the elementary fact that the number of dollars spent to purchase something necessarily equals the number of dollars received by the seller of that something. Thus, for the ith transaction in a particular period we have

$$\text{Purchase}_i \equiv \text{Sale}_i$$

The symbol "$\equiv$" means "identically true," or "by definition."

The same identity will obviously hold if we add up all the purchases and sales over a particular period such as a year. If there are n transactions over the year we have

$$\sum_{i=1}^{n} \text{Purchase}_i \equiv \sum_{i=1}^{n} \text{Sale}_i .$$

The purchases made during a year are made with a stock of money that turns over several times. For example, the money used in transaction i is transferred from the purchaser to the seller, and then the seller uses the *same* money in transaction j in which he or she is a purchaser. Thus, the sum of all the purchases in a particular period may be written as

$$\sum_{i=1}^{n} \text{Purchase}_i \equiv MV_T,$$

where M is the amount of money that is circulating and V_T is the transactions velocity of money—the number of times the money stock turns over in the year.

Now for the sales side of the identity. Each sale may be divided into price and quantity components,

$$\text{Sale}_i \equiv P_i q_i,$$

and this expression may be summed over all the sales in a year. While each individual transaction, in general, involves a different price per unit—after all, some of the units are apples, some are hours of labor, and some are shares of stock—we can in principle construct price and quantity indexes so that the sum of the dollar values of the transactions for a particular year is divided into two components, one reflecting the average price per transaction, P_T, and the other the quantity transacted during the year, T. Thus we can write

$$\sum_{i=1}^{n} p_i q_i \equiv P_T T.$$

When the results on the purchases side and the sales side are put together we obtain the famous equation of exchange:

$$MV_T \equiv P_T T.$$

The equation is written as an identity to reflect the fact that it has been derived from the original identity that purchases equal sales and that V_T, P_T, and T have been defined so as to retain the identity.

The equation of exchange *identity* becomes the quantity *theory* when three propositions are asserted to be true: (1) changes in the money stock do not change V_T; (2) changes in the money stock do not change T; and (3) with the money stock held constant, V_T and T change relatively slowly, or at least predictably, so that P_T won't change unless M changes. With these assertions the identity symbol in the equation of exchange may be replaced by the equals symbol. In this form the equation reflects the claim that changes in M will produce proportional changes in P_T.

There is a long history of controversy over the validity of the propositions that turn the equation of exchange from an identity to a theory. The major considerations may be briefly outlined.

Traditionally it was argued that transactions velocity is determined by the habits, customs, and payments technology of the community. The "custom" of a monthly rather than a daily paycheck clearly affects velocity, as explained earlier in the chapter. From that discussion, however, it is obvious that the frequency of payment is more than just a "custom"; the frequency depends, at least in part, on the costs of making and receiving payments and on the cost of holding money balances. These costs, although they depend on the rate of inflation which in turn depends on the rate of money growth, do not depend on the *level* of the money stock, but rather on relatively slowly changing preferences and payments technology. For example, automatic deposit of a paycheck into a checking account eliminates the need for a person to stand in line at a bank to deposit a paycheck. Thus it is not unreasonable to expect that transactions velocity would be relatively slowly changing and independent of the level of the money stock, although velocity might be affected during the period in which the money stock is changing from one level to another one.

This analysis suggests that we should not be surprised if transactions velocity drifts in one direction or the other over a long period of time. An important objection to the quantity theory, though, is that the total volume of transactions, T, is a concept that is both slippery and uninteresting.

That the concept is slippery can be seen by considering the effect on transactions volume of a merger between a food wholesaler and the retail grocery stores served by the wholesaler. Transactions between the wholesaler and the retailers are eliminated by the merger without there being *any* (or any significant) effect on the level of transactions with *final* users. Moreover, there may even be ambiguity about the very existence of intermediate transactions. An economic merger between the wholesalers and retailers may occur even though legally the retailers remain as separate corporations wholly owned by the wholesaler corporation.

That the concept of total transactions volume is inherently uninteresting can be seen by reflecting on some simple questions. Who cares if a can of beans is sold once or twice or three times after leaving the packing plant but before being sold to the final consumer? Can it really be that the price of beans, and of goods in general, depends in an important way on how many times beans are sold on the way to the final consumer? Isn't it more likely that if, in the equation of exchange, T should rise solely from a change in the number of intermediate transactions, then V_T would also rise so that there would be little or no impact on the general price level?

Glossing over these difficulties, let real GNP, y, be related to T by

$$y \equiv AT,$$

where $A < 1$ since the sum total of all transactions including intermediate transactions is larger than the sum total of all final transactions (the definition of GNP). And let the price index, P_y, appropriate for real GNP be related to the transactions price index by

$$P_y \equiv BP_T.$$

Using these expressions the equation of exchange may be written

$$MV_T \equiv \frac{P_y}{B} \frac{y}{A},$$

or

$$MV_y \equiv P_y y, \quad V_y \equiv ABV_T.$$

This expression gives the equation of exchange in its income form and the derivation shows how this form is related to the equation of exchange in transactions form.

The income form is the one underlying the discussion earlier in the chapter; the money stock per unit of real GNP—M/y—was related to the Wholesale Price Index which is highly correlated with the price index for GNP. The failure of M/y and P_y to move together perfectly may be interpreted within the identity form of the equation of exchange as reflecting variations in V_y or, within the quantity theory interpretation of the equation of exchange, the failure of the assertion of a constant velocity to be strictly true.

If the transactions version of the quantity theory were believed, the empirical evidence for the United States in Fig. 2.1 generates a puzzle. Money per unit of final output and prices have moved closely together, *very* closely together indeed after 1920. Given the enormous changes in the structure of American industry and in technology, belief in the transactions version of the theory implies an amazing stability of the parameters A and B in the formulation above. But another version of the quantity theory, that involving the Cambridge k, helps to explain the puzzle.

The Cambridge k

The Cambridge economists argued that the amount of real money balances people want to hold is a stable fraction of real income. Letting superscripts s and d indicate supply-and-demand functions, we have

$$\frac{M^d}{P_y} = ky, \quad \text{or} \quad M^d = kP_y y,$$

and

$$M^s = M,$$

where M gives the amount of money determined through the workings of the gold standard, by the government, or whatever. By adding the equilibrium condition that that amount of money demanded equals the amount supplied we obtain

$$M = kP_y y.$$

By comparing this expression with the one developed from the equation of exchange it can be seen that $k = 1/V_y$. The two formulations are alternative ways of developing the basic proposition that changes in the money stock per unit of real output cause proportional changes in the price level.

The ideas behind the Cambridge k help to resolve the puzzle discussed earlier. The emphasis on technology in the equation of exchange formulation suggests that velocity can be expected to rise, or k to fall, over time. For example, automatic deposit of paychecks should be expected to lead people to want to receive smaller paychecks more often rather than larger paychecks less often. But general improvements in technology raise the standard of living and provide families with more discretionary income—income over and above that which must be used to buy necessities.

One of the little luxuries in life is holding a larger average cash balance to avoid hand-to-mouth living and to have a ready reserve of purchasing power available to meet an emergency or to pick up a bargain. In discussing hyperinflation it was noted that a scarcity of real money balances develops—in the illustrative example average money balances went from four times daily pay to 0.4 times daily pay. People obviously feel worse off for losing the flexibility of deciding when to spend the fruits of each day's labor, and they do not sacrifice the flexibility unless the cost of holding money is high. These ideas may be formalized very conveniently using the Cambridge approach: the amount of money relative to income, k, that people want to hold depends on, among other things, the cost of holding money. When the cost is high, as in hyperinflation, k is small.

On the basis of the argument that k depends on the standard of living, velocity might be expected to fall gradually—k to rise gradually—as the general standard of living gradually rises. In fact, if this effect were most pronounced in moving from a near-subsistence to a comfortable standard of living, it would explain the declining trend of United States velocity before 1920 shown in Fig. 2.1. Careful study of the behavior of velocity in countries other than the United States may confirm or reject this conjecture.

Both formulations of the quantity theory provide insight into monetary processes. The Cambridge formulation has the advantage of being cast in a familiar supply-and-demand framework and stressing that the price level will depend on the supply of money relative to the amount people want to hold. The equation of exchange formulation, on the other hand, encourages explicit analysis of the technical factors that affect the amount of money people need and want to hold in the process of transacting the flow of business.

SUMMARY

In this chapter we have seen that the price level is closely related to the quantity of money in circulation, and changes in the price level to changes in the quantity of money in circulation. But for this relationship to be apparent it is necessary in some cases to make an adjustment to the data by expressing the quantity of money as a ratio to the level of real GNP.

In the United States the quantity of money relative to real GNP is closely related to the price level. The relationship is not perfect, especially on a year-by-year basis, but it is among the closest and most stable economic relationships known.

The basic reason for the close relationship between money and prices is that if the quantity of money that people hold suddenly jumps by X percent, then an increase in prices of X percent will leave them with an amount of money representing a command over the same amount of goods as before. If people were satisfied, given their options, with the initial size of their money balances in terms of command over goods, then they will also be satisfied if the quantity of money held and prices have both changed by X percent.

When prices are rising, as shown especially clearly by episodes of hyperinflation, it becomes costly to hold money because the money held buys less and less every day. Consequently, when prices are rising people tend to hold a smaller amount of money measured in terms of command over goods. In extreme cases, a severe scarcity of money adjusted for prices occurs because it is so very expensive to hold a reserve of purchasing power in money form. The greater the rate of expansion of nominal money, the lower will be the quantity of real money; stopping the printing presses will *increase* the real quantity of money in circulation.

These ideas, the quantity theory of money, may be formalized through either the equation of exchange or the Cambridge k approaches. In the equation of exchange the emphasis tends to be on the technical determinants of the velocity of circulation of money while the Cambridge approach emphasizes that for a given money stock the price level depends on the amount of money people want to hold.

REFERENCES

Cagan, Phillip, 1956. The monetary dynamics of hyperinflation. In Milton Friedman (ed.), *Studies in the quantity theory of money*. Chicago: University of Chicago Press.

U.S. Department of Commerce, Bureau of the Census, 1975. *Historical statistics of the United States: Colonial times to 1970*. Washington: U.S. Government Printing Office.

SUGGESTIONS FOR FURTHER READING

Dean, Edwin (ed.), 1965. *The controversy over the quantity theory of money.* Lexington, Mass.: D.C. Heath.

Graham, Frank D., 1930. *Exchange, prices, and production in hyperinflation: Germany, 1920–1923.* Princeton: Princeton University Press.

Money 3
and
Prices II

Given the discussion of the previous chapter, the reader might well wonder what more there is to say about money and prices. It certainly seems sensible to believe that when the quantity of something goes up its value must go down. Since a higher quantity of money is in fact associated with a lower purchasing power per unit of money, as demonstrated in the figures in Chapter 2, what more is there to discuss?

Monetarists in fact assert that 95 percent, or more, of the inflation story has been told in Chapter 2. But it takes only a little reflection to realize that there must be something about inflation that is highly confusing to many people. If the issue is so simple, why did the German people permit their government to increase the German money stock by almost 1 billion times in the early 1920s? The theory of inflation needs to be discussed carefully to identify the falacious arguments that lead governments to follow disastrously inflationary policies.

Before proceeding, one other point should be made. It was noted just above that it seems sensible to believe that when the quantity of money rises its value, or purchasing power, should fall. But if we use elementary supply-and-demand analysis, it is clear that this result holds only if the supply curve shifts out. If the demand curve shifts out while the supply curve stays put, then quantity and value both rise. To properly understand inflation, then, we must determine what factors are responsible for the shift in the supply of money function, and we must also consider the importance of shifts in the demand for money function.

In discussing changes in the price level we have already begun to use elementary supply-and-demand analysis; in the discussion in Chapter 2 the demand for money was related to the level of real GNP and the quantitative importance of this factor was stressed. It was emphasized that the amount of money people want to hold, on the average, depends on both the amount of business being transacted (the level of real GNP) and the prices at which goods and services are bought and sold. It was also stressed that the Cambridge k depends on the cost of holding money balances.

To isolate the effect of money on prices in the United States, therefore, we measured the money stock as a ratio to real GNP. But, as the figures in Chapter 2 made clear, even this method of measuring the money stock fails to produce an ironclad relationship between money and prices, especially in the short run. The importance of the short-run variability in money demand will be discussed fully in Chapter 7 on monetary policy. Here we merely note that the relationship between money and prices is much more stable in the long run than it is in the short run.

METHODS OF MONEY CREATION AND THEIR PRICE LEVEL EFFECTS

While the importance of output changes for money demand has been emphasized, the reasons for changes in the amount of money, the supply side, will be deferred until Chapters 6 and 7. But to better understand the implications of changes in the stock of money, in this chapter four different ways of changing the stock will be analyzed: (1) a currency reform; (2) a distribution of new money by a government mailing of 50 dollar bills to everyone; (3) a special government purchase of goods and services financed with new money; and (4) a government purchase of bonds from the public financed with new money.

Our purpose in examining these four ways of changing the stock of money is not to analyze the fundamental reasons why the money stock changes, but rather to discover whether the price level effects of money creation, or destruction, depend on the way in which a given change in the money stock is achieved.

Currency Reform Money

In 1960 the French government issued a new unit of currency called the "new franc." One new franc had a value equal to one-hundred old francs. To find the new franc price of an item all one had to do was to take the old franc price and move the decimal point two places to the left. The procedure was as simple as expressing prices in the United States in dollars rather than in cents: a price of 50¢ is easily converted to a price of $0.50.

When new francs were introduced prices, wages, rents, debts, and so forth were, in (new) francs, one-hundredth of what they had been, and the amount of money in circulation, measured by the number of (new) francs outstanding, was one-hundredth of the previous amount of money in circulation as measured by the number of (old) francs outstanding. The price level was obviously reduced by the same proportion as was the amount of money in circulation; any other result would have been most peculiar.

The principle underlying this example would hold just as well if the currency "reform" had gone the other way: one-hundred new francs issued for the old franc. Currency reforms never do take this form. Who wants to make all wages, prices, rents, debts, and so forth one-hundred times their old levels? But the principle is familiar from cases in which corporations have stock splits. In a typical stock split, each stock holder receives, say, two (new) shares for each (old) share owned. The stock price, the dividend, the per share earnings, etc., calculated on the new basis are exactly one half of their values calculated on the old, or presplit, basis.

It is easy to see why prices change by the same proportion as the number of units of money in circulation in a currency reform. But in the other methods of changing the quantity of money discussed below it is much easier to become confused. To reduce, if not avoid, confusion, the reader may find it helpful to define money quite literally—the paper currency and coin in the wallets, purses, pockets, and mattresses of a country's citizens. Bank deposits, which economists add to currency in constructing a formal definition of money, are, of course, close substitutes for currency, but in getting the theory straight it is frequently useful to assume that all deposits have been converted to "hard cold cash."[1]

Helicopter Money

Monetary theorists have long been interested in analyzing the effects of money dropped from the sky because, as will be seen shortly, this theoretical assumption avoids certain problems. Technological change has made life easier for the monetary theorist; it is much more efficient (less ink used) to speak of "helicopter money" than "money dropped from the sky."

As far as I know no government has yet distributed newly created money by helicopter, but there is a long history to proposals for the government to distribute newly created money directly to the population. Indeed, in 1975 the United States Government mailed checks to just about everyone in the country, calling the checks "tax rebates."

The 1975 rebate checks did not in fact represent newly created money because the government sold bonds to the general public to raise the funds. Taking the general public as a whole, people buying the new government bonds paid money into the government, and the government then mailed the money back out to the general public. But the rebate checks could have

---

1   To understand the importance of this definitional point, consider the following sentences: "He makes a lot of money." (Is he a counterfeiter?) "He ate up his inheritance in only three years." (Did he get indigestion?) To avoid confusion, speak of "earning income" and remember that one person's receipts of money are another's payments. The amount, or stock, of money in existence is not changed when money is transferred from one person to another.

represented newly created money (the government does have the power to create new money) and in this case we would have had a fine example of helicopter money.

Now consider what might happen if the government were to double the quantity of money over a very short space of time ("overnight") by putting the helicopters to work. How would this case differ from a reverse currency reform in which the government called in all the old dollars and issued two new dollars for each old dollar?

There are three important differences between the reverse currency reform case and the helicopter money case concerning *distribution effects*, the *price adjustment process*, and *anticipatory effects*.

To understand *distribution effects*, note that in the reverse currency reform case all claims and debts are automatically adjusted. If I owe the bank 1000 dollars, with the reverse currency reform I will now owe the bank 2000 (new) dollars. Similarly, my claims on others—my bank deposits, saving accounts, etc.,—will be restated in new dollar form. No such restatement occurs in the helicopter method of money creation.

In the helicopter money case we know prices are going to rise, but by how much? Suppose the helicopter distributes new money in such a way that each individual's and each firm's holdings of money are precisely doubled. Now suppose, for a moment, that all wages, prices, and rents doubled. Clearly, my dollar-denominated debts have been effectively cut in half, but so also has the value of all my assets that are denominated in dollars.[2] If my dollar-denominated debts equal my dollar-denominated assets, then I am neither better nor worse off when all wages and prices rise.

If my dollar-denominated debts are larger than my dollar-denominated assets, then I am better off when all wages and prices double. But, except for government bonds and debts owed by or to foreigners, every debt in the economy is someone else's asset. If I am better off by virtue of the doubling of all wages and prices, then someone else must be worse off.

In general, net debtors gain from the wage and price increases while net creditors lose.[3] If the creditors are, on the average, just like the debtors in

---

2 "Dollar-denominated assets (debts)" are those that promise (require) repayment of a stated number of dollars independently of what may transpire. Such assets are sometimes called "fixed-dollar assets" but this term is potentially misleading. For example, a United States Savings Bond has a schedule of values that rise over time; the dollars are not "fixed," but they are known at the time the bond is purchased and will not be adjusted in response to events after the time of purchase.

3 Actually, this proposition refers to *unanticipated* price increases. Precisely because debtors gain and creditors lose from unanticipated inflation, both groups have a powerful incentive to forecast inflation at the time loans are granted, and to adjust the interest rate on loans to reflect anticipated inflation. This important point is touched upon below and examined more fully in Chapter 5; for now, assume that all changes in the general price level are unanticipated.

terms of how they respond to being better or worse off, then all prices, wages, and rents can in fact double as assumed earlier, because the debtor's responses are cancelled out by the equal and opposite responses of creditors. When the effects of price increases on creditors and debtors cancel out, we say that in the economy as a whole there are no *distribution effects* from the price changes.

While important for many purposes, distribution effects do not appear to be of major importance in understanding the ultimate effects on prices of injections of helicopter money. If the money stock doubles, the average price level will in fact double, a little more or a little less, although some individual prices may change by a good bit more or less.

The second major difference between the reverse currency reform case and the helicopter money case is much more interesting. In a reverse currency reform the government tells us that each individual wage, price, rent, debt, etc. is to double, but with helicopter money we are not given this information. How do we discover what the correct prices are? What is the *price adjustment process*?

Let us analyze this problem in stages. Suppose we knew that the government distributed helicopter money in such a way as to double the money balance held by each and every individual and firm. We might then guess that as a first approximation every individual wage and price should double; for example, upon receipt of the information that the money stock had just doubled individuals might refuse to work unless their wage rates doubled, and firms might immediately double all their prices.

In general, however, not all individual markets would be cleared at these new prices. Suppose, for example, that creditors are on average wealthier than debtors.[4] In this case inflation has the distribution effect of making the wealthy poorer and poor wealthier. The demand for the luxury goods consumed by the wealthy will tend to fall and the demand for the necessities consumed by the poor will tend to rise. Thus, the prices of luxury goods will less than double and those of necessities more than double. This result, it should be emphasized, is fully consistent with the *average* of all prices—the price level—doubling.

Clearly, then, with helicopter money it may take some time for firms to find the correct prices. Similarly, workers in luxury goods industries may find that they cannot realize doubled wage rates because the demand for luxury goods is weak while those in other industries can realize more than

---

4   This assumption is being made solely for expositional purposes; whether inflation has a bigger impact on the rich or poor is a complicated question. While it may at first glance seem sensible to believe that creditors tend to be wealthy, note that corporations are substantial net debtors and that corporate stock ownership is heavily concentrated among the wealthy.

doubled wage rates because demand is strong. Moreover, the example being discussed has been deliberately "cooked" to make the problem clearer. Contrary to the assumption made above, the new helicopter money might all go to a few people, or might be distributed in equal per capita amounts; in either case the new money is not distributed proportionally to individuals' and firms' initial holdings of money, and so there may be distribution effects from the way the new money is distributed.

Finally, whatever the initial impacts on particular markets from the distribution of helicopter money, there will be further repercussions and adjustments over time. If luxury goods prices rise to a lesser degree than necessities' prices, then resources will tend to shift from the one set of industries to the other. Workers receiving lower wage increases will tend to be drawn to employments with higher wage increases. Those who were made relatively poorer will probably tend to save more to rebuild their net asset positions while those who were made relatively richer will tend to save less. All of these adjustments, however, will tend to reverse the original distributional changes and, therefore, the effects of those changes on particular wages and prices.

These adjustments will take time, but with the passage of time it is reasonable to believe that the helicopter money case will increasingly look like the reverse currency reform case. When all the dust has finally settled, individual wages and prices will have approximately doubled and certainly the average price level will be very close to twice what it had been.

Now we have our first example of why people may fail to associate increases in prices with increases in the quantity of money. When new money is distributed, the initial impacts on prices may be quite uneven. Some prices may be bid up dramatically, while others may change only slowly. Unanticipated increases in the money stock, the evidence suggests, have relatively little initial impact on the average level of prices. It is easy to interpret increases in individual prices as reflecting special conditions in particular industries rather than the early stages of a general price level adjustment.

But over time other prices do adjust as firms discover that higher prices will "stick" and as old contracts—including wage contracts—expire and are renegotiated at higher prices and wages. Is it any wonder that people fail to understand the link between money and prices? When money first increases unexpectedly, prices may not change much, and when prices finally do respond, the money stock may not be changing.

Figure 3.1 shows that this analysis is of more than academic interest. The figure shows the annual rate of inflation as measured by the Consumer Price Index and the annual rate of change of money per unit of output for quarterly United States data from 1947 through 1976. From this figure it appears that there is little or no relationship between money growth and the rate of inflation.

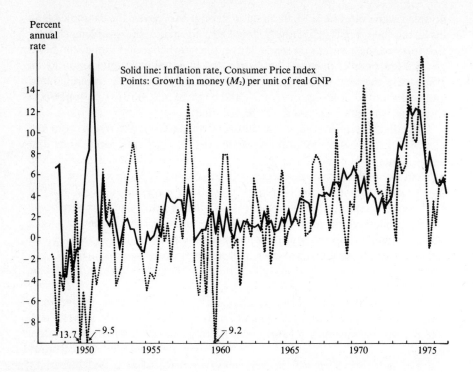

Percent
annual
rate

Solid line: Inflation rate, Consumer Price Index
Points: Growth in money (M_2) per unit of real GNP

Fig. 3.1 United States money growth and inflation, 1948–1976 (quarterly data).

But when the *levels*, rather than the rates of change, of the price index and of an index of money per unit of output are examined, the picture is very different, as shown in Fig. 3.2. This figure shows that, except for the extended period of adjustment following World War II, money and prices are closely related if allowance is made for an adjustment process of, perhaps, four to twelve quarters.

The adjustment process is complex because it involves changes in the level of output—booms and recessions—anticipations, the behavior of the monetary authorities, and other factors. In addition, the adjustment process may be affected by the imposition and removal of wage and price controls, currency devaluations or revaluations, and unusual events such as the OPEC oil price increases and embargo on oil shipments to the United States in 1973–1974. Because of the complexity of the price adjustment process, and its dependence on institutional detail of little theoretical interest, no effort will be made in this book to examine the subject in detail except with respect to the relationships between price and output adjustments discussed in Chapter 4.

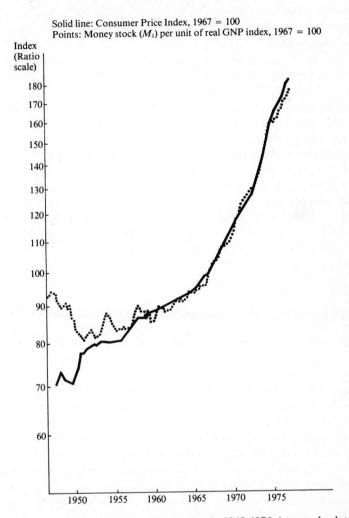

Solid line: Consumer Price Index, 1967 = 100
Points: Money stock (M_2) per unit of real GNP index, 1967 = 100

Fig. 3.2   United States money and price level, 1948–1976 (quarterly data).

In distinguishing helicopter money from currency reform money, two points have been emphasized so far. First, with helicopter money there will be distribution effects. If the money stock is increased unexpectedly, prices will rise and net creditors will lose while net debtors will gain. Second, with helicopter money the new wages and prices for all the thousands of different types of labor and products are not automatically announced as they are with currency reform money. It will take some time for people to find out what the new market clearing prices have to be.

A third important difference, not yet discussed, is closely related to the first two. If people learn when and how new money is being distributed, they will do their best to predict the impacts and obtain the largest possible gains or suffer the smallest possible losses. These *anticipatory effects* will alter the adjustment process.

Suppose, for example, new money were to be distributed proportionally to existing holdings. There would, obviously, be an incentive to increase the amount of money held just before the distribution date in order to obtain the maximum possible amount of the new money. One way to do so would be to sell some assets. But since the initial stock of money is fixed, everyone taken together cannot increase initial money holdings.

As people sell assets attempting to increase money holdings before the distribution date, the effect for all people taken together is not to increase their money holdings but to drive down asset prices. If the money stock is to be doubled, a bond that used to be worth $100 will be worth only $50 just before the new money is distributed. After the new money is distributed, the bond will be worth $100 again. With this result, a person with $50 before the new money distribution can hold onto it, receiving another $50 when the distribution takes place, or buy a bond for $50, which then rises in value to $100 when the distribution takes place.

This example illustrates an important principle: When values are expected to change in the future, prices will change in advance so that people will be indifferent between holding goods and money, given the anticipated changes in values. In the example above, people were indifferent between the bond and money only if the price of the bond dropped to $50. Similarly, to hold a real asset, such as a piece of land, people would have to expect that its price would double also, a reasonable expectation since the quantity of money is being doubled.

Ordinarily, however, new money is not distributed in proportion to the initial amount of money held. Knowing that prices will rise, people will want to convert their money into something useful before prices rise. But, in the society as a whole, the amount of money is fixed at any moment of time. The anticipation of rising prices in the future causes prices to rise immediately. How far will prices rise today? Prices will rise to the point at which people feel that equal value is obtained from holding either money or goods. The value from holding money is the value of the "money work" (discussed in the previous chapter) less the loss in purchasing power as prices rise. The value from holding goods is the services and enjoyment the goods yield.

In Chapter 2 it was noted that during hyperinflation prices get out ahead of money, and the real quantity of money falls. This pattern is quite evident in Figures 2.2, 2.3, 2.4 and 2.5. Judging from these figures, it looks as though the claim could be made that, since prices seem to move first, price changes cause money changes. There is a special sense, discussed in Chapter 7, in which this claim may be true, but the evidence in the figures does not necessarily support the claim. We have seen above how price changes can lead money changes not because price changes *cause* money changes but because people correctly *anticipate* money changes.

The importance of changes in the quantity of money in starting the inflationary process in Germany is shown in Fig. 3.3. The detail shown in this figure is completely lost in Fig. 2.2 because of the scale. Figure 3.3 shows that before hyperinflation started the money stock was rising persistently while prices were actually falling. This rise in the money stock, coupled with the growing realization that the money stock was out of control, finally produced the sharp price increases starting in mid-1921.

Deficit Money

Currency reform money and helicopter money have now been analyzed carefully, but the vast bulk of money creation takes different forms. One of these arises because governments frequently make expenditures not covered

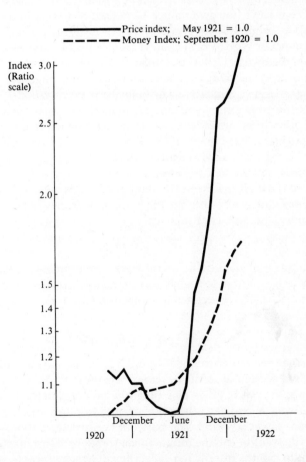

Fig. 3.3 The beginning of hyperinflation in Germany, September 1920–February 1922.

by tax revenues, and pay for those expenditures with newly created money. Since government expenditures minus tax revenues is the government deficit, this method of money creation may be called deficit money. The analysis of deficit money is more complicated than the analysis of helicopter money because the effects of changed government spending and taxes must be untangled from the effects of a changed money stock.

There is a much closer connection, however, between helicopter money and deficit money than might at first appear. Consider the following four cases: (1) to pay for an emergency defense mobilization, the government purchases new defense equipment with newly created money; (2) to pay for the mobilization, the government increases taxes; (3) the government buys new defense equipment, increases taxes, and then uses newly created money to rebate the tax increase to the poor; and (4) the government buys the new equipment and covers the cost by selling bonds to the general public.

In all four cases, the government has raised its expenditures. There is a budget deficit—expenditures greater than tax revenues—in all cases except (2). New money is created in (1) and (3), but not in (2) and (4). The key to sorting out these cases is the *government budget constraint*.

The government budget constraint reflects the relationship between inflows and outflows of government funds. It is *necessarily* true that every dollar taken in is used for something or, equivalently, that every dollar that goes out comes from somewhere. Government expenditures necessarily are financed through some combination of tax revenues, funds raised through the sale of bonds, and newly created money. Algebraically, if G is government expenditures, T is tax revenues, ΔB is the funds raised through the sale of new bonds (B itself represents the amount of bonds outstanding), and ΔM is new money creation (M itself is the amount of money outstanding), then the government budget constraint is

$$G \equiv T + \Delta B + \Delta M.$$

In this expression, M must be defined as "government-created money."

Now we can better see what is happening with deficit money. The government deficit, D, is defined as expenditures less tax revenues, and so we have

$$D \equiv G - T \equiv \Delta B + \Delta M.$$

Government expenditures can be financed by raising taxes as in (2). If taxes are not raised so that a deficit appears, then the deficit can be covered by issuing new money as in (1) or by selling new bonds as in (4). Case (3) might be regarded as a hybrid case; the government first raises taxes to pay for the mobilization—as in (2)—and then pays out newly created money making T smaller if you want to call the transaction a "tax rebate," or making G larger if you want to call the transaction "government expenditures to aid the poor (or the rich)."

Note also that if the government decides to obtain the funds for tax rebates by selling bonds, then ΔB is higher but ΔM isn't. When the bonds are sold, ΔM is initially reduced by the same amount but then is increased by the same amount when the rebate checks are mailed out, leaving no *net* change in the size of ΔM.

Helicopter money, as in a special tax rebate financed by new money issues, is clearly a type of deficit money. But for convenience let "deficit money" now refer to money created to pay for enlarged government expenditures.

The important question is the extent to which it matters, if at all, whether new government expenditures on military equipment are financed with taxes, bond issues, or deficit money. If the economy is fully employed, then resources will have to be bid away from some industries into those producing military equipment no matter what method of finance is used. Real GNP is reallocated, but the total not changed. (If the economy is not fully employed, then total real GNP may rise, a possibility discussed in Chapter 4.)

Suppose now that the deficit money is used to finance the emergency purchase of military equipment, but that the crisis is resolved and no additional equipment is purchased. After the crisis, the government budget returns to balance and involves exactly the same expenditures that would have occurred in the absence of the crisis. But the extra money—the deficit money—is still in circulation and will continue in circulation unless a positive step is taken to retire it.

If the money is not retired, then the situation is almost exactly the same as it would have been if helicopter money had been created. The *only* difference is that there is a stockpile of rusting military equipment sitting around and people have had to do without whatever goods were not produced because the resources were diverted to military equipment.[5] Once the economy has fully adjusted to the enlarged money stock, prices should be the same whether the money stock increase took the deficit or helicopter forms.

It is instructive to reexamine Fig. 2.1 showing United States money and prices. In World War II the money stock per unit of real GNP grew rapidly compared to the Wholesale Price Index, and the wartime monetary expansion was not reversed after the war. The price level then had some catching up to do, which it did during the Korean War speculative buying splurge in 1950–1951. In addition, after 1947 money growth was low relative to the growth in real GNP, and so money per unit of real GNP declined

---

5   It is just a bit too strong to say "*only*" because some of the resources devoted to military equipment production might be diverted from the production of capital goods such as machinery and factory buildings. Thus, the economy's productive potential might be lower.

somewhat. A similar story can be told about monetary expansion during the Vietnam War. During the war itself money per unit of real GNP rose more rapidly than prices, and then prices caught up in the 1973–1974 burst of inflation.

With deficit money the process of adjustment may be somewhat different from that with helicopter money. When helicopter money is distributed, the initial round of spending will impact a variety of markets whereas when deficit money is distributed the initial round of spending impacts particular industries—those producing military equipment in our example. But the differences are temporary because once the new money is in circulation it will be indistinguishable from previously created money and its ultimate effects on prices will not depend on how it was created.

Now suppose government spending is permanently higher, instead of only temporarily higher as assumed above. Suppose further that only in the first year of higher government spending is the extra spending financed by deficit money and that in later years the government raises taxes. The stock of money is permanently higher, as before, but does it matter that the level of government spending is permanently higher?

Whatever may be the effects of higher government spending, one frequently alleged effect—that of higher inflation—will not occur except, at best, and for reasons explained below, to a very minor extent. As long as the extra government spending does not generate extra money growth (and it need not if additional revenues can be raised), the rate of inflation cannot be affected. If the trend rate of inflation did rise, then the real money stock would fall year after year after year. But we have already seen that prices are closely related to the quantity of money per unit of real GNP. Government spending financed by taxes reallocates production, perhaps raising some prices and reducing other prices, but it does not change the trend rate of inflation.

The minor exception referred to above is that government spending can affect the inflation rate without affecting the rate of growth of money if the government spending changes the rate of growth of real GNP. If government spending is inefficient, then real GNP may grow a bit more slowly; for a given rate of growth of money, money per unit of real GNP will then rise. But government spending might increase the rate of growth of real GNP (by subsidizing research for example) in which case money per unit of real GNP will fall, or rise more slowly, and prices will tend to increase more slowly than they otherwise would.

If enlarged government spending is to increase the rate of inflation (other than to a small extent during the transition period over which resources are reallocated), then the enlarged spending must affect the money stock. Is such an effect likely? Maybe. Necessary? No. Most government spending is financed by taxes and there is no reason why all government spending cannot be financed by taxes.

Open-Market Money

The fourth method of money creation that needs to be examined may be called "open-market money." Referring to the government budget constraint again, $G \equiv T + \Delta B + \Delta M$, suppose G and T are held fixed but that the government enters the market for government bonds and buys some bonds for newly created money. The open-market terminology reflects the fact that private individuals and firms buy and sell billions of dollars of government bonds every day through government securities dealers, commercial banks, and other institutions, and when the government enters this open market its orders to buy or sell are treated as if they were private orders to buy or sell. In a purely private transaction, however, the parties to the transaction trade bonds for money, leaving the totals of both bonds and money held by the private sector as a whole *unchanged*. But after the government purchases some bonds, the private sector as a whole holds *fewer* bonds and *more* money. In the government budget constraint identity, ΔB is negative and ΔM is positive for the period in which the open-market transaction occurs.

This method of money creation (or destruction when the government sells bonds and takes money out of circulation) is of great practical importance since a separate agency of the government called the *central bank* has the power to engage in open-market operations in government securities. Although not all open-market operations change the money stock (for example, some central bank operations are designed to *offset* the temporary monetary impacts of actions by the United States Treasury in collecting and disbursing government funds), for present purposes it may be assumed that central bank purchases (sales) of government bonds do increase (decrease) the money stock.

After an open-market operation, or a series of such operations, the general public will end up with more money and fewer bonds, or vice versa. As emphasized earlier, it may take a substantial period of time before market prices fully adjust to the changed stock of money. In addition, the price adjustment process may reflect some distribution effects because both the stock of government bonds outstanding and the flow of annual interest payments by the government will have changed. But, as with other methods of changing the stock of money, there is no reason to believe that distribution effects and the adjustment process will affect the final equilibrium result to any appreciable extent.

Methods of Money Creation: Summary

The reader will no doubt feel that the simple picture existing at the end of the previous chapter has been so splattered with additional paint that the picture is no longer visible. Perhaps it is now clear how the disaster of the great German inflation could have occurred.

The argument above has been designed with one lesson in mind: no matter how the money stock is increased, prices will rise if the money stock per unit of real GNP rises. In some cases the price increases may precede the money increases and in other cases follow the money increases by many months, or even by several years. This is not to say that the equilibrium relationship between money and prices is exact; it is to say, rather, that general price increases that are *large* (whether in large steps over short periods or in a series of small steps over a long period of time) are monetary in origin.

Another point: monetary analysis is not all there is to understanding inflation. An understanding of why prices sometimes respond quickly and sometimes slowly to monetary changes is also of interest, although beyond the scope of this book. But there is a danger to be avoided. An extended analysis of inflation necessarily gets into detailed questions concerning the behavior of particular markets, adjustment speeds, formation of expectations, and so forth. The complexity of this analysis, and its success in explaining inflation in the short run, can lead analysts astray if they do not remember that these are just the details. Neglect of the monetary nature of inflation will lead to gigantic mistakes.

INFLATIONARY EQUILIBRIUM

The relationship of the price level to the money stock has now been explored fully. The reasons for the relationship have been analyzed, and so also have the reasons why the method of monetary expansion matters little. Now we will analyze a feature of some inflationary periods that puzzles many, and leads to distrust of the monetary explanation. That feature is the simultaneous appearance of inflation and unemployment.

It is intuitive to associate price increases with excess demand and low unemployment, which do indeed characterize many inflationary periods. But why should firms be raising prices when sales are weak, and why should wages be rising when many people are unemployed?

Suppose you were to accept a one-year job at a salary that you regarded as attractive, but then part way through the year found, to your dismay, that prices had gone up and your salary wouldn't buy as much as expected. And suppose, in addition, that friends with skills comparable to yours were landing jobs at higher salaries. You would be disappointed not only because your salary did not buy as much as expected but also because you would see that if you had waited a month or two you could have landed one of those better paying jobs.

And so, at the end of the year when your contract is up for renewal, you tell your boss that you'll quit unless your salary is raised to the levels your friends are getting. And suppose the boss says, "OK, I'll raise your salary," but that in the second year prices rise *again*, the buying power of your salary is lower than expected *again*, and your friends are getting better jobs *again*. What do you do when you negotiate your salary for the third year?

Now you're getting wise, and insist that your salary not only catch up to what others are getting, but also that a further boost be added to reflect your anticipations that prices and other salaries will be going up again. Your boss may agree if he or she expects that the prices the company can charge will also be going up. And if prices and salaries do go up about as expected, then everyone can be in equilibrium; at the end of the year no catching up need be done.

The notion of an *inflationary equilibrium* is very difficult for people to understand, perhaps because the typical person feels that the increase in his or her salary is fully deserved while the increases in prices are rip-offs. But if all these increases are anticipated, the inflationary equilibrium can be identical, or nearly so, to the noninflationary equilibrium. The same goods are produced and purchased, the same hours are worked, and so forth.

Consider the analogy of driving down an expressway at 55 mph. Clearly, you cannot be in equilibrium with an object 50 feet in front of you *unless* that object is also moving at 55 mph. You will be willing to go 55 mph following a truck by 50 feet only if you are quite sure that the truck won't be in the same spot a second from now. If your anticipations are not fulfilled, watch out. (Economies also crash when prices turn out to be much lower than anticipated, as discussed in Chapter 4.)

Now consider another analogy. Suppose 20 stopped cars were lined up on a track, all spaced 50 feet apart, and the drivers told that they were to accelerate rapidly to 55 mph holding the 50-foot spacing. If a signal were given, the cars could all start at once, but it is probable that, as during an accelerating inflation, some would get a little ahead and some a little behind. But suppose there were no signal. None of the cars could move very much until the first car did, and the tenth car, even if its driver saw the first car start, could not start until all the intervening cars had started.

When inflations accelerate the process is much the same. Some people get left behind, and some go too fast for a time; indeed the whole price level may get going too fast for a time. But inflations can settle down (at least moderate ones can) to a reasonably steady pace in which expectations are largely realized. The most serious problems seem to arise not from moderate inflation per se, but from unanticipated *changes* in the rate of inflation. As on both expressway and racetrack, it is the accelerations and decelerations that cause most of the trouble rather than the rate of speed itself.

Once everyone has adjusted to a given rate of inflation, the economy can function in almost exactly the same way as an economy without inflation. A sales decline in a noninflationary world leads a manufacturer to reduce prices; in an inflationary world the firm continues to raise prices, but not quite as rapidly as before. The expressway analogy is almost perfect. If you're in a parked car and a truck slowly backs up, you can avoid trouble by backing up too; if you're on an expressway and the truck in front slows, you slow but do not stop. In both cases the distance between the truck and your car falls, as may an economy's production and employment when its inflation rate falls. The intuitive feeling that inflation is necessarily linked to a booming economy is simply wrong.

Self-Generating Inflations

One last point: in theory, if prices start to rise and the money stock stays constant, the rising price level could induce continuous economization of cash balances (a continuing fall in the Cambridge k) so that the constant money stock could support higher and higher prices. In practice, this process never goes far enough to generate a hyperinflation. On the one hand, people realize that if prices stop rising, then the constant money stock will not support the high, but unchanging, price level. Knowing that prices will fall in this situation, people become cautious about buying goods whose prices, while currently rising, may be falling in the future. On the other hand, even without the damping effect of these anticipations, the economization of cash balances becomes increasingly costly. Perhaps prices can double fairly easily by people moving from monthly to semimonthly paychecks. But that prices will double again and again and again, with a fixed money stock, becomes more and more unlikely. How can cash balances be economized further once people are paid twice a day? Eventually more time would be spent shopping than working.

And so, prices do not in fact change substantially more rapidly, or slowly, for extended periods of time than the change in money per unit of output.

SUMMARY

This chapter has been devoted to a number of theoretical points that arise naturally in the context of explaining why the method of money creation makes essentially no difference to the effects of money on prices.

The effect of money on prices is most easily seen in the case of a currency reform. The number of units of money change and all prices change in exactly the same proportion. Other methods of changing the money stock differ in that they produce gains and losses for particular individuals. And, of course, the government may use money creation as a source of revenue that can be used to reduce taxes, expand expenditures, or retire government bonds held by the public. As capricious as the gains and losses from inflation usually are, they do little to affect the ultimate outcome on the average level of prices.

An essential aspect of understanding inflation is the concept of inflationary equilibrium. Once people have adjusted to an ongoing inflation, and have come to expect it, life goes on very much as though the inflation did not exist. During an inflation, firms can offer wage increases that would produce bankruptcy in a noninflationary world because they expect their prices to be rising and their unit sales to hold up even though prices are rising. During an inflation, firms that do not offer wage increases will lose their employees to other firms just as surely as would firms that cut their wages during a period of price stability.

In theory, inflation can be self-perpetuating without an increasing money stock. Expectations may force prices up. As prices rise, individuals want to hold smaller money balances, but since the total quantity of money is fixed, attempts to hold less money simply drive prices higher. This theoretical possibility seems not to be important empirically. If people have confidence that the money stock will not increase, then they know that a speculative bubble in the price level cannot continue long. From the United States experience it does not appear that a self-generating inflation could take the price level more than a few percent above the level warranted by the quantity of money per unit of real GNP.

Money   4
and
Output

In this chapter the task is to understand the relationship between money and fluctuations in the total output of the economy, the real GNP. The level of output is, of course, produced by the employed portion of the total labor force, and so fluctuations in the level of output (or, more precisely, in the level of output relative to full employment output) will be reflected in fluctuations in the rate of unemployment.

In the long run, output is completely, or almost completely, independent of the level of the money stock and of its rate of growth. Abstracting from short-run business cycle fluctuations, the output of an economy is determined by the size of the labor force, its productivity, and the size of the capital stock. These factors are influenced very little by the long-run behavior of the money stock.

The main interest, then, in this chapter will be the study of short-run fluctuations in output or what is commonly called the "business cycle." It should be emphasized, however, that business fluctuations are not in fact cyclical in the sense of a regularly recurring phenomenon such as ocean waves; business fluctuations are irregular and not "cyclical" in any proper sense of that term. Nevertheless, because the word "cycle" was long ago attached to the phenomenon of fluctuations in business activity we shall sometimes lapse into that terminology because it is so familiar.

MONEY AND BUSINESS FLUCTUATIONS
IN THE UNITED STATES

In the United States the relationship between fluctuations in the money stock and fluctuations in business activity may best be described by sketching the course of a "typical" business cycle. Suppose that the money stock has been growing smoothly and that the level of business activity has been growing smoothly (reflecting growth in the labor force, in productivity, and in the capital stock) at approximately full employment levels. The price level is increasing at the same rate as the money stock per unit of real GNP, and people have become accustomed to that rate of increase. Now suppose that the rate of growth of the money stock declines. Initially it is found that the rates of growth of both prices and output are unaffected. However, in the space of six to twelve months business activity begins to decline. At this stage of the business cycle, near the business cycle peak, it is sometimes the case that the rate of growth of the money stock declines further, a pattern especially characteristic of severe recessions. As the money growth rate continues to fall, business activity continues to fall and unemployment rises.

After a time, money growth stabilizes, or perhaps turns up. The business cycle recovery begins a few months later and, if the money stock growth rate remains stable, the business recovery will proceed. We are now back to the beginning of the story and the stage is set for a new decline in money growth to start the movement toward another business cycle peak.

The picture just outlined is a very stylized one, but it nevertheless gives the main flavor of United States experience. To see this picture graphically for the last two United States business cycles, the relationship between money and unemployment is shown in Fig. 4.1. The trend rates of growth of the money stock during the business expansions ending in 1969 and in 1973 are shown as solid lines. Careful examination of the figure will show quite clearly the typical pattern in which the money stock drops below its trend before the business cycle peak.

Two different definitions of the money stock are shown in Fig. 4.1: M_1 is currency in the hands of the nonbank public plus the public's demand deposits at commercial banks while M_2 is M_1 plus time deposits, other than large negotiable certificates of deposit, at commercial banks. In studying United States prices the M_2 definition was used because the M_2 data series is available for a longer period of time and because M_2 seems to be slightly more closely related to prices than is M_1. But in studying business activity there seems to be little to choose between M_1 and M_2, and so both are shown.

One other aspect of Fig. 4.1 deserves mention. Following the monetary deceleration in 1969, money growth returned to approximately its previous rate shortly after the November, 1969, business cycle peak, as can be seen from the fact that the gap between the money stock and the trend line stays about constant in 1970. The 1969–1970 recession was relatively mild, consistent with the fact that the monetary deceleration did not continue during the recession. In contrast, money growth fell significantly after mid-1974—the cycle peak was in November, 1973—a fact consistent with the 1973–1975 recession being relatively severe.[1]

---

1   For charts showing money and business cycle back to 1907 using the same techniques, see Poole 1975.

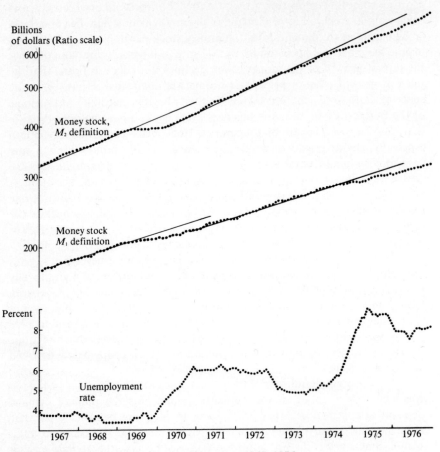

Fig. 4.1 Money growth and unemployment, 1967–1976.

In spite of the fact that the relationship pictured in Fig. 4.1 is well established (practically every recession in United States history displays the same pattern[2]) the reasons for the pattern are subject to hot dispute. In describing Fig. 4.1, therefore, mention of cause and effect relationships was deliberately avoided. But when cause and effect relationships are discussed below, keep in mind the pattern in Fig. 4.1.

---

2   The possible exceptions that require the word "practically" are the 1937–1938 and 1948–1949 recessions. For both of these recessions the cycle peaks *were* preceded by monetary decelerations, but the peaks occurred so long after the decelerations that they might be regarded as exceptions. See Poole 1975.

THE PROBLEM OF CAUSATION

In attempting to understand the relationship between money and business cycles there is a serious problem concerning the direction of causation. In discussing the relationship between money and prices we were able to make use of a very simple and very solid theory. That theory involved the proposition that if the money stock were to double, then the doubling of all prices would leave everyone in exactly the same real situation as before (except for distribution effects). And it was easy to spell out the nature of the economic forces that would raise prices following a doubling of the money stock. But when talking about the relationship between money and business activity, there is no simple theory to which we may appeal.

One of the key problems in interpreting the evidence, such as that presented in Fig. 4.1, is that we can never be absolutely sure whether the change in the money stock caused the change in business activity, or the change in business activity caused the change in the money stock, or some third factor caused both. It might be the case, for example, that toward the end of a typical business cycle expansion something happens, something that we do not understand at the present time, that sets in train a series of events leading both to the decline in business activity and to the decline in the money stock.

In principle, the same argument could be made concerning the relationship between money and prices. Perhaps price increases cause money increases. But from both theory and evidence we know that whenever a nation tolerates a monetary system in which price increases cause money increases, the result is high, or even hyper-, inflation. And we know that when a causal connection going from prices to money is broken, the inflation stops. The business cycle relationship is much less well understood, in part because there has never been a long period of absolutely steady money growth. If such a period were available, it would be possible to observe directly whether business cycles would occur in the absence of monetary fluctuations.

Although the direction of causation is not easy to sort out, much can be said. If changes in business activity caused changes in money, then we know that the money changes would have to take place through a mechanism that somehow operates on the behavior of the banks and banking authorities. We know that the central bank (the Federal Reserve System in the United States) could as a technical matter prevent the money stock from following a path such as the one shown in Fig. 4.1. If the Federal Reserve permits a particular monetary fluctuation to occur, we can explore the reasons why.

In attempting to provide evidence on the causation question we have no choice but to look for certain natural experiments. In a natural experiment we look for cases in which nature causes a certain variable to fluctuate for identifiable reasons, and look for results to show up in other variables. By identifying the causes of particular monetary disturbances, we can build a case that for *those* disturbances we know the cause and know that it was *not* a business cycle fluctuation. There can, of course, always be disagreement about whether a natural experiment has been identified and whether, in any particular case, the causation is in fact running from the money stock to output, but the general approach is certainly useful.

There are enough cases from history to suggest that the causation in general does run from the money stock to output. Particularly good examples arose during the gold standard years before the Federal Reserve System was established. There were times when gold discoveries produced very large amounts of new gold flowing into the monetary system of the country. Surely in such a case it is farfetched to argue that the gold discoveries were caused by a third factor that also caused the business cycle itself. When gold discoveries took place, the effects expected from the basic theory actually were observed fairly promptly.

As another example, ever since Keynes published his famous *General Theory of Employment, Interest and Money* in 1936 it has been common to argue that changes in government spending and taxes rather than monetary fluctuations are important in the business cycle process. Because newly created money has so often been used to finance government budget deficits, it has been argued that the government budget is the cause, at least in some cases, of both the business cycle and the monetary fluctuation, with the monetary fluctuation *itself* playing a small role in the cycle.

This hypothesis is difficult to test because fluctuations in the government budget and the money stock have so frequently occurred together. In fact, if budget fluctuations and monetary fluctuations *always* went together it would be impossible to disentangle their separate influences. However, budget and monetary fluctuations have not always occurred together and so the hypothesis can be tested.

Two dramatic examples of government budget and monetary fluctuations in opposite directions occurred in the 1960s. In 1966 money growth fell abruptly while government spending on the Vietnam War was rising sharply. The outcome of these opposing forces was a *slowing* of economic activity. Real GNP actually fell in the first quarter of 1967. Money growth then resumed and so did the inflationary boom. In mid-1968 a tax increase went into effect but money growth continued unabated and the boom did *not* slow. The slowdown did not come until after money growth decelerated in 1969. Perhaps some other third factor was important in these two episodes, but at least we know that the assertion that monetary changes are correlated with the business cycle *only* through the government budget deficit mechanism is wrong.

The direction of causation issue has been discussed here because it is central to the monetarist argument that monetary fluctuations are causes and not effects. This is not to say that monetary fluctuations are uncaused (of course *something* causes the monetary fluctuations themselves), but that the relationships between money and prices, and between money and business activity, are such that *if* the money stock were kept stable by the central bank or some other arrangement, *then* fluctuations in prices and business activity would be far smaller than those observed historically. Let us now examine the reasons why monetary fluctuations cause business cycle fluctuations.

THE MONETARY THEORY OF THE BUSINESS CYCLE

In discussing the business cycle the common starting point of all monetary theorists has been to emphasize that changes in the money stock produce what may be called "transitional" fluctuations in business activity. These transitional periods, which may be many years long, arise in the process of people adjusting from one rate of growth of the money stock to another. As seen in Chapters 2 and 3, one of the adjustments required is that of getting the price level to rise at the new rate required by the new rate of growth of money. In the short run, prices do not ordinarily adjust completely because it takes time for buyers and sellers to determine the new set of prices required to clear markets. If prices do not adjust completely, then we have good reason to believe that output will be affected over the period of adjustment. These transitional periods may be regarded as characterized by mistakes because goods are bought and sold at incorrect prices and on the basis of mistaken expectations as to future changes in prices and other variables.

The Demand for Money

To make the argument more precise, the key concept of the demand for money needs to be discussed at greater length than it was in Chapter 3. To understand the basic ideas, ask yourself the following questions: How much money do you hold on the average? And why? In thinking about these questions most people will realize that they use money to bridge the gap between the time when they receive payments (wages, salaries, rents, dividends, interest, and so forth) and the time when they make payments. Money is also needed to serve as the medium of exchange. Only money is acceptable by the shopkeeper; assets such as common stock and government bonds are not accepted in payment, but must first be sold for, or converted into, money and the money then used in payment. Therefore, the amount of money that is held on the average is related to the sizes of the streams of income and payments *and* to the extent to which receipts and payments are synchronized. This point was emphasized in the discussion of hyperinflation; synchronization is close indeed when workers are paid twice a day.

Why do people not synchronize their receipts and payments perfectly? Why do people not spend their paychecks the moment they are received? Of course, people do tend to spend more on payday, but obviously they do not spend their entire paychecks on payday. And the reason is simple. There are many things that must be purchased close to the time that they are used. The paycheck which arrives at the end of the month may be used to buy certain things that can be stored (canned goods, for example) but there are other things that cannot be stored, such as fresh vegetables, haircuts, and seeing a movie that has not yet come to town. A paycheck cannot be converted immediately into all the things and services that will be purchased, but funds must be put into some form of "holding pattern" to be available when needed. Individuals typically hold a reserve of purchasing power in some combination of currency and demand deposits, but now another question arises.

Why is the reserve of purchasing power not held in some form of asset that earns interest and then the interest-bearing asset converted into money just before going to the store or the movie? Here, again, introspection will make clear the basic reason. It would be a terrible nuisance to have to run to the savings bank to obtain money before every trip to the store. It is more convenient to withdraw several days' worth of money at a time in order to reduce the number of trips to the bank. Similarly, if we think about the possibility of investing the paycheck in the stock market, it is clear that the brokerage cost might completely wipe out any earnings that might be obtained from having funds invested for a short period of time.

These considerations may be summarized by saying that money functions as a generalized means of payment, a medium of exchange, and as a temporary abode, or reserve, of purchasing power. From the general considerations discussed it is clear that: (1) the higher a person's income, the higher the average level of money balances that will be held; (2) the higher the cost of converting money balances into earning assets and back again, the higher will be the level of money balances held; and (3) the more costly it is to hold money, the greater the extent to which the costs of more closely synchronizing receipts and purchases and of temporarily investing in earning assets will be worth bearing and the lower will be the level of money balances held.

Now we may use a simple example to aid our understanding of money demand. Suppose you work 40 hours a week at $3.60 per hour for a total of $144 per week. Out of that $144 per week income, suppose that on average you hold $45 in cash. For example, when you receive your paycheck at the end of the week, you might spend $54 and then have $90 left that you then spend in equal installments of $15 each day over the next six days. In this way your average holding of money is $45.

Suppose, alternately, that you work 36 instead of 40 hours, but at a wage of $4.00 per hour instead of $3.60. In this case weekly earnings will also be $144. Is there any reason to believe that the average amount of money held will be different from the previous example? The answer is probably not, or not by very much. (With a 36-hour week you have more time to economize on money balances by making trips to the savings bank and so you might hold a bit less.) So we may conclude that as a first approximation the average amount of money held depends on the level of money income and not separately on the wage rate and the number of hours worked.

When viewing the amount of money held in relationship to the flow of income, it is natural to speak in terms of the concept of velocity—the ratio of the level of nominal income to the average level of the money stock in a particular period. In the example above, income for the week was $144 and the average level of the money balances held were $45, yielding a velocity of 3.2. In fact, this example involves money balances much lower than are actually held. In the United States the level of M_2 velocity has long been about 2.5 but with respect to the *annual* rather than the *weekly* rate of income. Much of this money is, of course, held by business firms rather than by individuals. The inverse of velocity (about $\frac{1}{3}$ in our example) is a convenient measure of the amount of money people hold per unit of nominal income, the Cambridge k.

Effects of a Monetary Contraction

Now let us consider a thought experiment. Suppose that the subject of the experiment is a man working steadily 40 hours per week, earning $3.60 per hour for a total of $144 per week. Now suppose that the man wakes up one morning and finds that his money balance has been cut by $4.50, or 10 percent. Instead of having $45 in his bank account in the middle of the week, the man finds the account contains only $40.50. He has not been robbed, let us say, but $4.50 has been invested automatically in a savings account. And we will assume that a similar occurrence happened to everyone else in the economy.

Given that the man's cash balance is down, but that the funds are in a savings account, what he does is go to the savings bank to withdraw $4.50 to put back into the demand deposit account. However, everyone else in the economy is trying to do the same thing. Where do savings banks obtain the money to meet the withdrawals? They obtain the funds by writing checks on *their* demand deposits.

If everyone together tries to take money out of savings banks, what must happen is something along the following lines. The savings banks, given that everyone is trying to get money out, find that to satisfy their depositors' demands they have to reduce the amount of their mortgage lending, or perhaps they have to sell some government bonds. As they reduce mortgage lending, people are unable to buy the houses they had planned to buy. As savings banks sell government bonds, bond prices decline and some people are persuaded to delay some of their purchases of goods in order to take advantage of the low bond prices. As people reduce their postponable purchases of items such as clothing in order to put the funds into government bonds, the firms that make such goods find that the demand for their products has declined. Similarly, those refused mortgage loans cannot buy new houses, and so those who build houses and make the equipment for houses find their sales have declined. The hours worked by people in industries facing declining demands must, therefore, fall.

Suppose, furthermore, that with the 10-percent cut in the money stock, the prices of goods and the hourly wage rates paid labor are initially unchanged. Then, it will no longer be possible for everyone to be employed for 40 hours per week. Instead, the average hours of work must decline because the amount of money in existence will not support the same flow of *nominal* income as before. Thus a 10-percent reduction in the quantity of money will produce a 10-percent reduction in the flow of nominal income; if wages and prices are fixed in the short run, then all of this reduction in nominal income will take place through a reduction in real income. A 10-percent reduction in the number of hours worked will change hours of work from 40 hours per week to 36 hours per week, and at the wage rate of $3.60 per hour the total flow of income will be $129.60 per week, exactly 10-percent below the previous income of $144 per week.

Review the steps in this thought experiment for a moment. It was initially argued that an income of $144 per week arising from 40 hours of work at $3.60 per hour would generate the same demand for money as would an income of $144 per week arising from 36 hours of work at $4.00 per hour. The average money balance of $45 was held because it was convenient to do so. Holding a smaller average balance required greater efforts at synchronizing receipts and payments, and the benefits of holding smaller balances (the interest earned on investing the extra funds or the enjoyment of goods purchased with the extra funds) were not worth the extra bother required when smaller balances were held. Thus it was established that the demand for money depends as a first approximation on nominal income and not separately on the wage rate and hours worked components.

The final step of the argument was to note that *if* the money stock declined by 10 percent and *if* the wage rate were unchanged, *then* nominal income would have to fall by 10 percent by having the number of hours of work fall by 10 percent. Once nominal income has fallen by 10 percent the amount of money demanded will also have fallen by 10 percent, matching the fall in the supply of money. Once nominal income is down, people will no longer want to withdraw funds from savings accounts for the purpose of adding to demand deposit accounts.

It is clear that if a way could be found to reduce all prices and wage rates, then nominal income could fall by 10 percent without a fall in hours worked. The requirement is for the wage rate to drop by 10 percent to $3.24 per hour. That wage rate at 40 hours per week involves an income of $129.60, down 10 percent from $144.

The numbers in this example are illustrative only, because money demand is not a constant fraction of nominal income; in fact, some economization of money will be induced by the higher interest rates following the cut in the money stock and the relationship between money and nominal income fluctuates for other reasons which are not well understood. But the basic empirical validity of the argument was demonstrated in a different guise in Chapter 2. In Fig. 2.1 it was shown that the price level is closely related to money per unit of real GNP. To see the links let Y be current dollar GNP, y be real GNP in 1967 dollars, and P be the price index defined on a 1967 base. To construct Fig. 2.1 each annual observation of M/y was divided by the constant required to make M/y for 1967 equal 100. Call this constant C. Thus Fig. 2.1 shows that

$$P \approx \frac{M/y}{C}, \text{ or}$$

$$V = \frac{Y}{M} = \frac{Py}{M} = \frac{P}{M/y} \approx \frac{1}{C},$$

where the symbol "$\approx$" means "approximately." Clearly, if velocity were strictly constant, then the Cambridge k $(= \frac{1}{V})$ would be a constant and equal to C. A feeling for the accuracy of the approximation may be obtained by looking at Figs. 2.1 and 3.2 again, or by referring to Fig. 4.2 which reproduces a chart from the Federal Reserve's *1977 Historical Chartbook*.

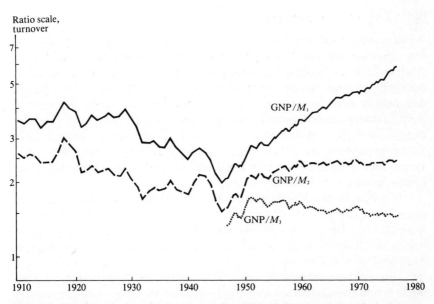

Fig. 4.2 Income velocity of money annually, 1910–1946: seasonally adjusted, quarterly, 1947–1976.

Figure 4.2 shows velocity measures calculated from the M_1 and M_2 measures of the money stock and from the M_3 definition of the money stock—M_2 plus mutual savings bank deposits, savings and loan shares, and credit union shares. While different economists have different attitudes as to which definition is "best," for many purposes it makes relatively little difference which definition is used. For example, if the upward trend in M_1 velocity after World War II is accounted for, then the relationships of M_1 to GNP and of M_2 to GNP appear about equally reliable and stable. However, the uncertainty about the reasons for the postwar trend in M_1 velocity and, indeed, for the historical fluctuations in velocity however defined, make clear the importance of not claiming too much for the monetary theory of nominal GNP. On a very short-run basis, fluctuations in GNP have, historically, been as much a result of fluctuations in velocity as in the money stock.

The simple example discussed and the evidence on velocity provide a feel for the closeness of the relationship between money and *nominal* income. It is clear, then, that the key to understanding the relationship between changes in the money stock and business activity (the level of *real* income) is an understanding of the factors that prevent prices from adjusting quickly in the short run in response to monetary disturbances. Some of the relevant considerations were discussed in the previous two chapters, but in those chapters the slow adjustment of prices was discussed primarily from the point of view of the relationship between money and prices and not the relationship between money and business activity.

Short-Run Price Adjustment

A little thought will make clear the reasons why most prices and wages do not adjust quickly except during periods of hyperinflation. Many individuals work under wage contracts specifying the wage rates for a contract period of one or more years. In some cases labor contracts are for two or three years, and only in extreme circumstances will they be renegotiated before they expire. Sales practices involving commitments to sell at list prices, prices in printed catalogues, and so forth, are common. Firms do not change these prices instantaneously, in part because of the cost of printing new catalogues, and in part because they feel a commitment to sell at the advertised prices customers have come to accept.

The fact of incomplete short-run price and wage adjustment is clear enough and so also are the manifestations of slow adjustment in the form of contracts, catalogue prices, and so forth. But the question is *why* business is conducted under such arrangements. A number of different explanations have been offered. For many years the explanations concentrated on factors such as labor unions' habitual behavior, the customs of the society, and so forth. But as more is learned about these phenomena it becomes increasingly clear that economic explanations should be sought for most price rigidities. The general approach is to compare the benefits and costs of changing wages and prices to the parties involved.

As an example, consider the pricing of restaurant meals. Suppose you are interested in dining out on a Saturday night, but you want to go to a moderately priced restaurant. If restaurant prices don't change very much from one week to the next, your choice can be made on the basis of information derived from past experience, conversations with friends, and advertising. Information collected over a substantial period of time will be relevant and useful, and it will not be necessary to make a lot of telephone calls Saturday afternoon or to visit a number of restaurants Saturday evening before deciding which one to select. In short, price stability in this industry reduces the cost of the consumer accumulating needed price information. The same argument holds for stability in the quality of the product and service.

Consider an alternative pricing system in which a restaurant changes its prices substantially from one day to the next. You call to find out this Saturday's prices, but have to wait because the telephone is busy. Or you drive to the restaurant, park, and check the prices on the menu posted in the window, knowing that the prices may be too high for you that day and you may want to go on to another restaurant. Or, you decide the hassle is not worth the trouble and you strike the restaurant from your list. If many people respond this way, the restaurant loses many potential customers and may find that to stay in business it is forced to adopt a stable pricing policy. The restaurant must balance the benefits of the increase in demand resulting from a pricing policy that reduces the costs of customers obtaining information against the costs of sometimes selling steak at a loss because meat prices have risen sharply.

It is worth taking this example one step further. If meat prices fluctuate enough, the stable pricing policy will break down. If meal prices are to be held stable in this case, the restaurant would have to set the price of a steak dinner high enough to limit its losses when the price of steak happens to be very high. But a competing restaurant might then introduce a variable pricing policy. The possibility of getting a steak dinner for several dollars less would attract customers. The information that "steak is a real bargain this week at restaurant X" might spread fairly rapidly.

Pricing policies do in fact change over time as a result of considerations such as those just discussed. Indeed, within the same restaurant policies may differ for different types of meals. It is common for the price of lobster dinners to fluctuate substantially and not to be printed on menus because the price of lobster fluctuates so much depending on the size of the catch. On the other hand, the prices of other dinners are printed on menus and change relatively infrequently.

Pricing stability, then, makes good economic sense for some types of goods. But the consequence of pricing stability is that demand shifts do not initially affect prices. A restaurant does not raise its prices if business is especially good some particular Saturday night; business is sometimes good and sometimes not so good, but "averages out." If a demand shift persists, though, and business is good night after night after night, then prices may be raised. The first good night will not bring the price increase because the restaurant owner has no way of knowing that the first night *is* the first of a string of good nights rather than a temporary fluctuation in business. It is easy to see how price changes will lag behind changes in the state of business.

It should be emphasized that *uncertainty* is the key to sluggish price response and not resistance to price changes per se. Movie prices change a lot from Saturday night to Tuesday afternoon; so also do Miami hotel prices from January to July. These price changes do not cause the difficulties discussed earlier because information on the price changes is available in advance to moviegoers and vacationers. Price changes *per se* do not impose information and planning costs on prospective buyers, but *unpredictable* prices do. The essential point is not that prices don't change but that they respond slowly to unforeseen changes in demand.

This same argument applies to wage rates as well as prices, and applies with even greater force. Before changing jobs individuals want some assurance about the wage rates they are to receive. This assurance may be embodied in a formal contract, or take the form of a set of business practices and understandings.

Knowing that price and wage decisions will be binding, to a greater or lesser extent, for a period of time, the parties involved will do their best to set prices and wages at the most appropriate levels. For firms making pricing decisions, "appropriate" means "profit-maximizing"; for individuals and firms bargaining over wages, "appropriate" again means "profit-maximizing" for firms, and means "utility-maximizing" for individuals. These decisions, of course, are made in the context of opportunities available elsewhere in the labor and product markets.

THE THEORY RESTATED

Now the various threads of the argument may be pulled together. For the reasons discussed, wages and prices are typically set in advance. For some things, like lobster dinners, "in advance" means only a few hours before the restaurant opens for the day; for other things, like labor, "in advance" may mean three-year contracts. Changes in economic conditions will change these practices; in hyperinflation the three-year labor contract may become a one-week contract. But in the context of fairly stable general prices, as in the United States, "in advance" means a substantial length of time in many markets.

As unforeseen changes in demands occur, prices and wages do change, but not immediately and not all at once. The consequence of this pricing behavior is shown in Fig. 4.3. For the industry depicted, firms have set prices that cluster around P_0. These prices were set in the expectation that demand would be D_e, and if demand turns out as expected firms

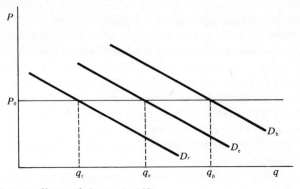

Fig. 4.3 Output effects of demand shifts.

will be producing quantity q_e. At q_e marginal cost (not shown) equals price, and profits are maximized.

If demand is unexpectedly low at D_r, as in a recession, or unexpectedly high at D_b, as in a boom, price will remain at or near P_0 until firms have had time to respond. Therefore, recession output is q_r, and boom output is q_b. Why does demand change unexpectedly? Because the money stock falls (rises) unexpectedly and individuals, directly or indirectly, reduce (increase) their demands for goods as they try to adjust their money balances.

If the money stock has fallen so that demand shifts to D_r, a sufficient drop in price will restore output to q_e. For the representative, or average, market the price must drop by the same percentage as the money stock declined. This decline in price, along with the declines in wages that are also required, will take time, and over that period of time output will be less than normal, a recession. But eventually the correct price will be found and output will return to q_e.

STAGFLATION

A situation in which the economy is slumping, or stagnating, at the same time inflation is continuing has come to be called "stagflation"; however, such a situation might just as well be called "inflump." Whatever it's called, there's no doubt that the situation is uncomfortable.

Economists have been accused not only of not knowing how to cure stagflation but also of not knowing how to explain it. The first charge is true if by "cure" is meant a remedy that is "fast, safe, and effective." The second charge is simply false. Indeed, not only are the reasons for stagflation understood, but the same analysis with signs reversed explains the situation opposite to stagflation—a booming economy with relatively stable prices, or "staboom." The key to this analysis is the concept of inflationary equilibrium which was explained toward the end of Chapter 3.

A situation of inflationary equilibrium in which the money stock is rising steadily and in which everyone has become accustomed to rising prices is shown in Fig. 4.4. In period 1 firms in the representative industry depicted *expect* demand to be D_1, they set price at P_1, and *realized* demand is D_1. In period 2, *expected* demand is D_2, price is set at P_2, and *realized* demand is D_2; and similarly for period 3. For simplicity, the quantity q_e, which is both the expected and the equilibrium quantity, has been shown as unchanging over time, but it would obviously be a simple matter to incorporate a growing q_e into the argument.

The inflationary equilibrium can continue indefinitely so long as expectations of rising prices are realized. To slow the inflation, the rate of money growth must be reduced. If the reduction occurs in period 3, the realized demand in period 3 will be lower than D_3 in the figure. Output will decline, as will employment, *even though prices are rising*. The situation will be one of stagflation.

If inflationary expectations are solidly entrenched, in period 4 firms may raise prices by just as much as before even though period 3 output was unexpectedly low. Firms may well reason that the relatively low demand was just a temporary aberration. It is normal for demand to fluctuate around the level expected, and this situation is not changed by virtue of being in an equilibrium at an inflation rate of 10 percent rather than one percent. Thus, the stagflation may continue for some time.

A continuing situation of weak demand, however, will convince more and more firms and workers that lower rates of price and wage increase are needed for levels of output and employment consistent with efficient operation and individuals' employment goals. This realization will spread firm by firm, union by union, person by person; and as it does and as old contracts expire lower rates of increase of prices and wages will be established. There is no reason for these rates of increase to drop immediately to zero; employing the analogy used in Chapter 3, as traffic congestion increases it appears

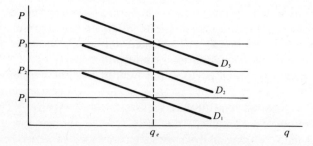

Fig. 4.4 Prices and output in an inflationary equilibrium.

appropriate for the driver to slow down from 55 mph to, say, 45 mph, but not to jam on the brakes and come to a full stop.

When we look at the data, then, what we should expect to observe is that periods of above normal unemployment are associated with declines in the rate of inflation. The rate of inflation itself may be uncomfortably high, but the rate should be falling. And this is the pattern we actually observe.

Figure 4.5 shows the three stagflation episodes that have attracted the most attention by observers of the United States economy, the 1957–1958, 1969–1971, and 1974–1976 periods. The contraction phase of 1957–1958 business cycle lasted from mid-1957 to the spring of 1958 as can be seen in the figure from the rising unemployment rate over these months. The inflation that started in early 1956 continued unabated through most of the downturn, but then slowed abruptly in early 1958.

In contrast to the 1958 experience, in 1970–1971 inflation slowed very gradually in response to the 1969–1970 recession, but the inflation did slow as the reader may confirm by placing a straightedge on the chart of the Consumer Price Index in 1970–1971. The same method may be used to verify the slowing of inflation in 1975–1976 in response to the 1973–1975 recession.

It is certainly true that the decline in the inflation rate in the second and third of the episodes being examined was painfully slow. Indeed, impatience with the progress being made in 1971 was responsible for the adoption of general wage and price controls in August of that year, which is why Fig. 4.5 was drawn with the 1968–1971 episode stopping with the July, 1971, observations for the price index and unemployment rate.

Some will scoff at charts such as Fig. 4.5, saying that a microscope is needed to detect the slowing of inflation in 1971 and that the slowing in 1975–1976 was due to the fact that the OPEC oil cartel was no longer raising oil prices so rapidly. Neither argument is satisfactory.

In assessing the validity of scientific propositions about how the world works, what biologist would scoff at a professional colleague who uses a microscope? The slow response of inflation may well have policy significance (a matter examined in Chapter 7) but it has nothing whatsoever to do with the proposition that a slowing of money growth slows inflation through a process that (ordinarily) includes a recession. And with respect to the OPEC argument, one (but not the only) reason oil prices rose less rapidly in 1975 was that a worldwide recession weakened the demand for oil and made it in the best interests of the cartel to raise oil prices at a slower rate.

There is, of course, the interesting and important question as to why the decline in the inflation rate was so slow in 1970–1971 and 1975–1976 compared with 1958, and it must be admitted that a completely satisfying answer is not available. But the evidence is consistent with the sensible proposition that the longer an inflation lasts, the more deeply embedded will be institutional manifestations of inflation and inflationary expectations.

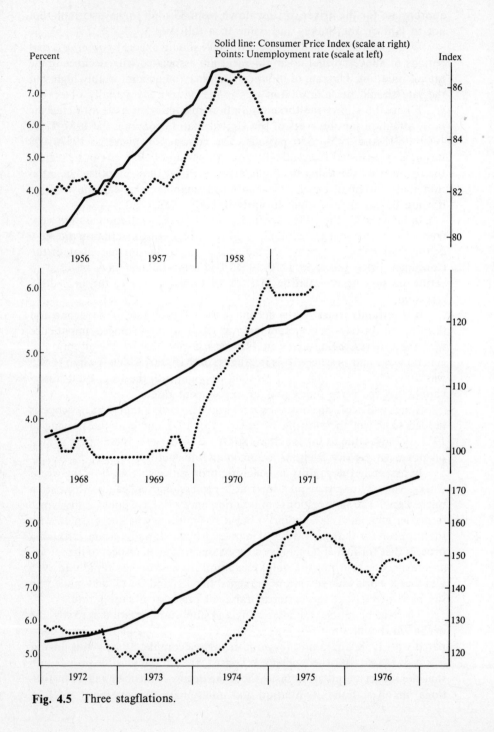

Fig. 4.5 Three stagflations.

In studying the 1958 experience it must be noted that the CPI was actually falling at the end of the 1953–1954 recession, and continued to drift ever so slightly down until mid-1955. Thus, the inflation preceding the business cycle peak in mid-1957 had lasted only about a year and a half when the recession came along.

By 1970, however, the Vietnam War inflation was five years old. The inflation had begun in early 1965 and, except for a modest slowing during the minirecession of 1967, had not only been continuing but also worsening steadily. In the twelve months ending December, 1964, the CPI rose by 1.2 percent; the corresponding figure for 1965 was 1.9 percent; in 1966, 1967, 1968, and 1969 the increases were 3.3 percent, 3.2 percent, 4.7 percent, and 6.0 percent, respectively.

Against this background it is not surprising that the mild 1969–1970 recession did not generate a quick slowing of inflation. And by 1975 the situation was even worse; the slowdown in inflation in 1972 had been followed by CPI increases of 8.9 percent in 1973 and 12.1 percent in 1974.

While this argument is sensible it is not completely satisfying because so little is known about the details of the formation of expectations. The argument is not, for example, consistent with the rapid transition from inflation during World War I (an inflation that lasted from 1915 through 1919) to actual deflation in 1920–1921. Perhaps the World War I inflation was regarded as a special event associated with a major war; perhaps adherence to the gold standard at that time produced convictions that the inflation would not continue. Unfortunately, we just don't have solid evidence either to support or to disprove these propositions.

In summary, stagflation is an uncomfortable phenomenon but it is not inconsistent with the monetary theory of the business cycle. In some cases it does take a microscope to support the theory, but when the microscope is properly focused there can be no doubt about what is being seen. Weak demand does lead to a slowing of inflation. It is clear that the monetary cure to inflation is sometimes "slow and effective"; whether it is "safe" is another matter, to be discussed in Chapter 7.

NONMONETARY CAUSES OF BUSINESS FLUCTUATIONS

The analysis of the mechanisms by which monetary disturbances cause business fluctuations can be used to study the effects of disturbances other than in the rate of growth of money. Several such disturbances will be considered.

Shifts in the Demand for Money

If the demand for money changes, so that people want to hold more (less) money at any given level of nominal income, then the effects on business activity will be the same as those when the supply of money falls (rises). An attempt by people in general to hold larger money balances must fail when the supply of money is fixed, but the attempt will reduce bond prices and spending on goods and services, producing a business downturn.

Although the matter is subject to considerable dispute between monetarists and nonmonetarists, monetarists interpret the available evidence as showing that the demand for money is stable, and that shifts in the demand for money are quantitatively of little importance compared with shifts in the supply of money. Much of what appears to be instability in the demand for money, monetarists argue, in fact reflects lagged adjustments to prior instability in the supply of money.

Shifts in the Demand for Goods

Figures 4.3 and 4.4 show that any *unexpected* shift in demand, no matter what its cause, will produce a change in output. If, for example, the demand for cars declines because consumers are concerned about the possibility of a sharp increase in gasoline prices, then the production of cars will fall.

A decline in the demand for one product, however, means little or nothing for business activity in general. Consumer demands are always shifting from one product to another, and so outputs of some products are falling while others are rising. When automobile demand falls, the demand for air travel may rise. Total, or aggregate, demand is what matters for general business activity.

In forecasting shifts in aggregate demand it is far too easy to overestimate the impact of highly visible disturbances to particular industries. Fears concerning future gasoline prices may produce a dramatic and highly visible shift away from cars offset by a large number of small, practically invisible, shifts toward other goods. To avoid overestimating the aggregate impacts of highly visible disturbances, this question should always be asked: "Will consumers simply save the funds that would have been spent on good X in the absence of the disturbance?" Before answering "yes," ask whether the unspent funds will just sit quietly in pockets without burning any holes. Don't most people want so many things they cannot afford that reduced expenditures on cars will lead them to buy other items on their wish-lists?

One other aspect of this problem should be considered. If consumers do reduce their total spending, the unspent funds will be invested in savings accounts, bonds, and so forth. The extra funds being saved will tend to reduce interest rates. Lower interest rates will persuade some people to borrow money to finance purchases of items such as houses, cars, TV sets, furniture, vacations abroad, and so forth, items frequently bought on credit. Lower interest rates will also encourage business firms to borrow funds to finance new factory buildings, machinery, and so forth. Thus even if there is a decline in aggregate consumption demand, there will be a partial offset as lower interest rates encourage larger demands for investment goods. However, the offset is likely to be less than complete in the short run because at lower interest rates the cost of holding money is lower and so the Cambridge k will probably be higher. Over time the offset will be more complete because extra real money balances will be generated as weak markets cause price shading.

Here again the evidence is hotly disputed, but monetarists believe that aggregate demands are not highly unstable, and that whatever instability may exist is offset to a very substantial extent by interest-induced changes in the interest-sensitive components of aggregate demand.

Price Disturbances

Another nonmonetary disturbance that in principle could be important may be analyzed by returning to Fig. 4.3. Suppose the economy is in a noninflationary equilibrium, with prices stable at P_0 in the representative, or average, market because firms expect demand to remain at D_e. Realized demand is not absolutely constant, but fluctuates randomly around D_e and firms have no reason to change their demand expectations.

Now suppose that firms, for some reason, suddenly feel that demands will rise, and so prices are raised above P_0, say to P_1 (not shown in Fig. 4.3). If demand does not in fact rise above D_e, then output will fall to the quantity given by the intersection of a horizontal line at P_1 and D_e. The price expectations disturbance has caused a recession.

Disturbances of this type appear to be quantitatively unimportant for a not unsurprising reason. Recall that in Fig. 4.3 firms set P_0 so that at output of q_e marginal cost equals P_0, the profit-maximizing operating rule for firms. Any firm that frequently sets price above or below P_0 will make below-normal profits, and perhaps suffer losses. In the latter case it eventually goes out of business; in the former, it is a ripe target for a takeover by another set of managers who will avoid the pricing mistakes.

In any event, the evidence is fairly strong that, if anything, firms adjust prices too slowly rather than too rapidly. With an exception about to be discussed, the case for an important independent role of price disturbances is weak.

The exception, or possible exception, is the large oil price increase engineered by the OPEC oil cartel in late 1973 and 1974. The increase was quantitatively significant, and it occurred so quickly that there was insufficient time for downward adjustment of other prices to prevent the general price level from rising. And since the business cycle peak occurred in the fourth quarter of 1973, the argument that the OPEC oil price increase caused the 1973–1975 recession has great appeal. Note, however, that the OPEC oil price increase did not reflect faulty expectations of rising demand but exploitation of previously unused monopoly power.

While the OPEC oil price increase surely tended to work in the direction discussed, its quantitative importance is difficult to estimate because a typical monetary deceleration was occurring at the same time, as can be seen by taking another look at Fig. 4.1. Only if the monetary deceleration had not occurred would we have had some reasonably clear evidence. At a minimum, it must be accepted that the monetary deceleration made the recession worse than it otherwise would have been, and it is quite possible that without the monetary disturbance the OPEC oil price increase would have had only a minor impact on business activity.[4]

MONEY AND OUTPUT IN THE LONG RUN

Monetary surprises are related to business fluctuations, but a sharp distinction should be made between high money growth and variable money growth. If money has been growing at four percent and then starts to grow at six percent, there will be a surprise during the transition from four to six. But in time people will learn that the new rate of money growth is six percent. And as they learn, and if there are no further monetary surprises, business activity can return to its full employment level.

The situation is more complicated when we have unstable money growth. Suppose that money growth varies as with the flip of a coin, being sometimes high and sometimes low on a random basis. There will necessarily be some surprises all the time. But now suppose that money growth fluctuations become even larger. Money growth might vary as with the flip of a coin, but with variations twice as large as before. The surprises will be larger and the effects on business activity will be larger.

Nevertheless, when money growth becomes more variable there are many things that business firms and households do to adjust their normal practices to reduce the impact of monetary instability. For example, with zero inflation and relatively stable money growth we observe frequent use of long-term price and wage contracts. When inflation rises but is still fairly stable, we find that the contracts provide for rising prices and wages over time to reflect the expected inflation. If inflation becomes more volatile and unpredictable, then cost-of-living escalators that automatically adjust wages for the amount of inflation are included in labor contracts. If the unpredictability rises further, contracts may be shortened from, say, three years to one year, or wage-reopener clauses may be written into contracts. And going to

---

4   It may be noted that the monetary disturbance was more complicated than just the deceleration after mid-1973. The substantial acceleration of money growth in 1972 pushed the economy into an unsustainably rapid expansion, and pushed employment temporarily above the full employment level. Thus even if money growth had remained constant after mid-1973 and the OPEC price increases had not occurred, unemployment would have increased in 1974. The monetary deceleration was certainly enough to turn this adjustment into a recession without the OPEC oil price increase.

the extreme, wage contracts in hyperinflation may be compressed to one week and workers paid twice daily. Firms post prices on a blackboard instead of printing price lists and may give up mailing dividend checks because the rate of inflation is so high that the erosion in the purchasing power of the dividend while it is in the mail makes it not worthwhile to attempt to send dividends to shareholders.

Many of these changed business practices are costly but do not show up as reductions in GNP. Resources are shifted from previously productive uses to new uses required to deal with the high and variable rate of inflation. But for moderate inflation this diversion of resources does not appear to be at all serious. Thus a long-run inflation, if steady and anticipated, probably has very little impact on the level of real activity and its growth over time. Indeed there may even be some benefits from inflation in the long run, although those benefits are easily overestimated. One possible benefit is that the government raises a certain amount of revenue by printing money, revenue that would otherwise require tax collectors. The substitution of money revenue for tax collector revenue obviously reduces the cost of government because tax collectors cost more to hire than printers do.

SUMMARY

Monetary fluctuations are related to business fluctuations in a systematic way. Starting from a position of full employment equilibrium, a decline in the rate of money growth drops the level of the money stock increasingly below its previously established trend. Six to twelve months after the decline in money growth, business activity peaks and a recession begins. At this time money growth sometimes declines further, producing an especially deep recession.

Once money growth stabilizes, conditions conducive to the end of the recession develop. In a few months the business cycle trough occurs and the economy begins the recovery phase of cycle. This phase continues, and accelerates if money growth accelerates, until another monetary deceleration sets the stage for another business cycle peak.

The process by which monetary fluctuations cause business cycle fluctuations is complex. One part of the process involves attempts by people in general to replenish (unload) their money balances once the money stock has fallen below (risen above) its established trend. These attempts push interest rates up (down) and reduce (increase) the demand for interest-sensitive goods and for goods and services in general.

These changes in demand catch firms unaware, and since prices have been determined somewhat in advance by firms' expectations of demand, the deviation in demand from expected initially shows up in an output fluctuation and has very little impact on prices. Over time, however, firms learn that the demand changes are not just temporary. As their demand expectations adjust, they change prices and the price changes work in the direction of restoring normal full-employment output.

The impact of a monetary fluctuation, therefore, shows up first in a changed level of business activity, and only later in prices. The adjustment process extends over several years, and so the price and output changes observed one year reflect the cumulative impact of monetary disturbances and the adjustments to them over the previous several years. The speed with which the adjustment takes place depends on a variety of factors, and is clearly compressed as conditions become more unstable as during a hyperinflation.

Causes of business cycle fluctuations other than money supply disturbances exist, but are of limited quantitative importance. These causes include shifts in the demand for money, in the demand for goods, and in prices and price expectations. These shifts, which play an important part in the process by which monetary fluctuations cause business fluctuations, appear to play a very limited *independent* role. The author's guess as to their quantitative importance is that in the United States after World War II independent nonmonetary disturbances have accounted for unemployment fluctuations of about 0.5 percentage points on either side of the normal full-employment level of unemployment (which has itself changed over time for a variety of reasons). Over the same period unemployment has actually fluctuated in a range of roughly two percentage points below and three percentage points above full-employment norms. Thus, most of the fluctuations in unemployment have been due to monetary instability.

REFERENCE

Poole, William, 1975. The relationship of monetary decelerations to business cycle peaks: another look at the evidence, *Journal of Finance* **30** (June): 697–712.

SUGGESTIONS FOR FURTHER READING

Friedman, Milton, and Anna J. Schwartz, 1963. Money and business cycles, *Review of Economics and Statistics* **45**, Supp. (February): 32–54.

———, 1963. *A monetary history of the United States: 1867–1960*. Princeton: Princeton University Press, especially Chapter 7, The great contraction, 1929–1933, and Chapter 13, A summing up.

Lucas, Robert E., Jr., 1977. Understanding business cycles. In Karl Brunner and Allen Meltzer (eds.), *Stabilization of the domestic and international economy*. Amsterdam and New York: North Holland.

Money 5
and
Interest Rates

In this chapter the relationships between money and interest rates are explored. For the most part these relationships are indirect. Money growth affects the inflation rate and the level of economic activity, both of which in turn are major determinants of the level of interest rates. In addition, when the rate of growth of money changes, but before inflation and economic activity are affected, there may be some direct monetary impact on interest rates, but this impact is probably relatively small.

As the reader is no doubt aware, there is an enormous variety of interest rates—rates on short- and long-term securities, on government bonds and corporate bonds, on savings accounts and home mortgages, and so forth. In the analysis presented here, the focus will be on interest rates on high-grade securities, but for the purposes at hand it is not necessary to be very precise about exactly what interest rates are being analyzed. As Figs. 5.1 and 5.2 make clear, interest rates on various types of securities fluctuate very much together. While much can be said about the determinants of interest rate differentials, our concern will be with the broad movements of interest rates in general.

THE SIMPLE ARITHMETIC OF INTEREST

A thorough understanding of the simple arithmetic of interest is essential to an understanding of the economics of interest. The arithmetic is, fortunately, very simple although calculation is sometimes tedious.

The best place to start is with the concept of *future value*. If $100 is placed in a savings account at five percent interest for one year, then the amount of interest earned will be $5. Assuming the interest is left in the account, at the end of the year the account balance will be $105. Or, in symbols,

$$A_1 = A_0(1 + i),$$

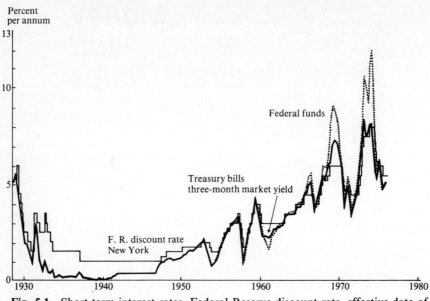

Fig. 5.1 Short-term interest rates. Federal Reserve discount rate, effective date of change; all others, quarterly averages.

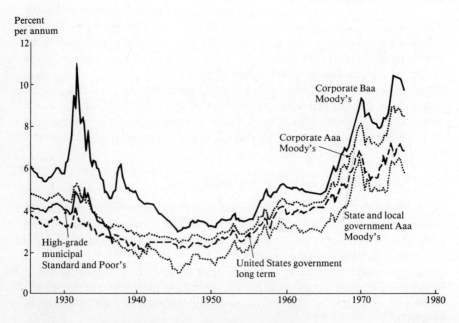

Fig. 5.2 Long-term bond yields, quarterly averages.

where A_1 is the account balance at the end of the year, A_0 the balance at the beginning of the year, and i is the interest rate expressed in decimal rather than percent form. This formula gives the *future value*, A_1, of A_0 dollars invested for one year at the interest rate i.

When funds are invested for more than one year, the same formula may be applied year by year as many times as needed. For example, it is obvious that $A_2 = A_1(1 + i)$. But since $A_1 = A_0(1 + i)$, we have $A_2 = A_0(1 + i)^2$. Thus the formula for the future value of A_0 dollars invested for two years at the same interest rate i is

$$A_2 = A_0(1 + i)^2.$$

Similarly, the future value of A_0 dollars invested for n years is

$$A_n = A_0(1 + i)^n.$$

Now the concept of *present value* may be explained. If the interest rate is five percent, how many dollars are needed *now* in order to have $105 available in one year? The answer, obviously, is $100; $100 is said to be the present value of $105 in one year at five percent interest. In symbols,

$$A_0 = \frac{A_1}{1+i}.$$

This formula can be obtained by simply dividing both sides of the future value formula by $1 + i$. Similarly, the present value of A_n dollars in n years is given by $A_0 = \dfrac{A_n}{(1+i)^n}$. Another frequently used terminology is that A_0 is obtained by discounting A_n; the *discount factor*, $(1 + i)^n$, is divided into A_n to obtain A_0.

Since the concept of present value so frequently seems confusing, one further comment may prove helpful. Whenever confusion reigns, start with the future value formula: "If I invest A_0 dollars now at i percent for n years, I will end up with $A_n = A_0(1 + i)^n$. If I know A_n, then I can find A_0, the present value of A_n, by dividing both sides of this formula by $(1 + i)^n$."

This discussion has been based on the assumption of *annual compounding*: it was assumed that interest was added to an account at the end of each year. In the analysis below annual compounding will be assumed; no essential difference is made by the fact that in practice a great variety of compounding periods are employed in interest rate calculations.

THE FOUR TYPES OF LOANS

There are four basic types of interest-bearing accounts and securities: the savings account, the bill, the bond, and the mortgage. Most people are familiar with the savings account—interest is added to the account every year (or every quarter, or every month) and if no withdrawals are made the account balance will grow over time according to the future value formula discussed above. Obviously, the higher the rate of interest, the more rapidly the account balance will grow.

The essential characteristic of the savings account is that the account balance is fixed at any moment of time and variations in the rate of interest generate variations in the amount of interest earnings. The present value is certain while the future value is unknown and subject to variation as the interest rate varies.

Unlike the savings account, bills, bonds, and mortgages all have known future values while their present values change when interest rates change. Consider first a one-year bill. The borrower promises to repay $100 in one year. In return, the lender turns over to the borrower the present value of $100 in one year, $100/(1 + i). The bill, whether a piece of paper with fancy engraving, an IOU on a scrap of paper, or a computer entry, may then be sold by the original lender to someone else. If the interest rate has gone up (down) between the time the original loan was made and the bill is sold, the present value of the bill goes down (up). The borrower is unaffected; his or her promise is to repay $100 at the maturity of the bill *regardless* of what might happen to the interest rate.

Loans in the form of bills, sometimes called discount loans, are ordinarily limited to relatively short maturities, usually a year or less. Longer term loans take the bond or mortgage form. In a bond the borrower promises to pay a predetermined *dollar* amount of interest every year and then to repay the principal at the maturity date. A mortgage has exactly the same form except that the principal is repaid year by year along with the interest instead of in a lump sum at maturity.

Consider the example of a $100, 20-year, five-percent bond. The annual interest payment is five dollars. This interest payment is fixed at the time the bond is sold and does not change over the life of the bond no matter what happens to market rates of interest. The interest rate written into the bond agreement is frequently called the coupon rate since in most cases the bond owner clips coupons off the bond year by year and sends them to the borrower in order to get the annual interest.

The present value of the bond is nothing more than the sum of the present value of all the coupons and the principal repayment. The first coupon, C, has a present value of $C/(1 + i)$, the second $C/(1 + i)^2$, and so forth out to the last coupon which has a present value of $C/(1 + i)^{20}$ on a 20-year bond. Thus, the present value of a bond maturing in m years is

$$PV = \frac{C}{1+i} + \frac{C}{(1+i)^2} + \cdots + \frac{C}{(1+i)^m} + \frac{100}{(1+i)^m}.$$

This same formula can be used to calculate the present value of a mortgage except that the annual mortgage payment, in dollars, is substituted for C and the last term representing the lump-sum bond principal repayment upon maturity is deleted.

From the present value formula for a bond (or mortgage), it is clear that the value of a bond will fluctuate if the market rate of interest, i, fluctuates. As emphasized in discussing bills, fluctuations in the market rate of interest do not affect borrowers' obligations on outstanding bonds or mortgages. For example, most readers are aware that the payments on home mortgages are not affected by fluctuations in market interest rates, a consequence of the mortgage form of borrowing.[1] But fluctuations in market rates of interest do affect the market value of the mortgage and therefore affect the lender.

The characteristics of the principal forms of loans have now been outlined along with the simple arithmetic of interest rates. The key point to understand is that when funds are borrowed through issuance of a bill, a bond, or a mortgage, the dollar repayment obligations of the borrower are fixed and do not change over the life of the loan. Changes in market rates of interest do, however, affect the owners of outstanding bills, bonds, and mortgages. An increase (decrease) in the market rate of interest decreases (increases) the present values, and therefore the market values, of these securities.

REAL VERSUS NOMINAL INTEREST RATES

The discussion so far has concerned *nominal* interest rates—interest rates stated in money terms without allowance for changes, if any, in the general price level. But the importance of inflation is obvious; would you rather lend $100 for one year at five percent in the United States today or 100 marks for one year at ten percent in Germany in 1922? Clearly, lending funds in Germany at ten percent in 1922 was essentially equivalent to giving money away since the purchasing power of 110 marks in 1923 was a tiny fraction of the purchasing power of 100 marks in 1922. If the inflation rate is 300 percent per month, then a nominal interest rate of 300 percent per month is required just to stay even, to maintain the *real* value of the funds lent.

The relationships between the real rate of interest, the nominal rate of interest, and the rate of inflation can be seen as follows. First, note that the real rate of interest is five percent if a loan yields enough dollars so that after one year five percent more goods can be purchased even though goods prices have changed. For example, if corn costs $2.00 per bushel, $200 will buy 100 bushels. One year later the price of corn may have changed, but if a $200 loan plus the interest earned will buy 105 bushels, then the real rate of interest, r, is five percent.

Real interest rate calculations are not ordinarily made using the prices of particular goods but, instead, using a general price index. If P is the price

---

1 The type of mortgage being discussed here is the fixed rate mortgage; variable interest rate mortgages, though not common, do exist.

level at a particular time, then PX dollars are required to purchase X units of goods in general at that time. If $P + \Delta P$ is the price level one year later, then $(P + \Delta P) X (1 + r)$ dollars are required to purchase $X(1 + r)$ units of goods one year later. The dollar *amount* of interest is the difference between $(P + \Delta P) X (1 + r)$ and PX. The nominal interest rate, i, expressed in decimal rather than percent form, is the dollar amount of interest divided by the loan of PX dollars. Thus,

$$i = \frac{(P + \Delta P) \; X \; (1 + r) - PX}{PX} = r + \frac{\Delta P}{P} + r\frac{\Delta P}{P}$$

As long as the inflation rate and the real rate of interest are both relatively low, the term $r\dfrac{\Delta P}{P}$ is very small and may be neglected. Thus, the frequently used relationship $i = r + \dfrac{\Delta P}{P}$ is obtained. This relationship is often written $r = i - \dfrac{\Delta P}{P}$ to reflect the fact that once a loan has been made at a stated nominal interest rate, i, the real rate of interest actually earned will depend on what the inflation rate turns out to be.

THE EFFECTS OF INFLATION ON INTEREST RATES

Now that interest rate arithmetic and background have been discussed, let us begin the discussion of interest rate economics by examining the effect of long-run inflation once the economy has fully adjusted to inflation. To understand the effect of inflation on the nominal rate of interest, consider the following example: Suppose, first, that the long-run rate of inflation is zero and that the rate of interest charged on a car loan is eight percent. Suppose, further, that the price of the car is $5000 if purchased today and, because there is no inflation, the price of the car is expected to be the same next year. Finally, suppose that you expect to receive a $5000 inheritance next year and that you expect to use $5000 to buy a car. The question is this: Should you borrow $5000 today to buy the car in order to be able to enjoy it for a year, expecting to repay the borrowing in one year with the inheritance, or should you wait and simply buy the car next year?

To examine this question, consider two alternative courses of action. If the car is purchased today and $5000 is borrowed, then with the interest rate of eight percent on the car loan the interest expense is $400. Suppose, for the sake of argument, that $400 sounds fairly costly to you given your current need for a car and you are just on the borderline as to whether you should pay the $400 in order to enjoy the car now or whether you should wait for a year to avoid paying interest. In the language that economists so often use, you are *indifferent* between buying the car now and buying it later.

To make this decision in an inflationary period we need to examine the same kinds of numbers. But in the inflationary period we know that the price of the car will be higher next year by, say, five percent. Thus, the car that can be purchased for $5000 this year is expected to cost $5250 next year.

If the nominal interest rate on the car loan is still eight percent, then it clearly pays to buy the car now if you were indifferent in the situation when there was no inflation. With the eight percent rate of interest you must still pay the $400 of interest but you save the $250 price increase by buying the car this year instead of next year. The net interest cost is only $150 from buying the car now; if you were just indifferent before when it cost you $400, then clearly you will buy the car now when the net interest cost is only $150. This net interest charge of $150 on the $5000 of borrowing works out to an interest rate of three percent instead of eight percent. In other words, the real, or inflation-adjusted, rate of interest is now three percent.

What would the nominal interest rate have to be in the inflationary situation for you to be indifferent between buying the car now and buying it later? Suppose the interest rate on the car loan were 13 percent instead of eight percent. Then, on the $5000 loan the interest expense would be $650 whereas it had been $400 before. However, paying the $650 interest allows you to avoid the $250 price increase, leaving a net of $400, the same as before.

This example conforms to the simple formula derived earlier for calculating the real rate of interest: the real rate is the nominal rate less the rate of inflation. It is quite clear that should you anticipate inflation, you will regard the nominal rate of interest in a different way from the way you would regard it if you do not anticipate inflation.

In this example we have discussed the *demand for borrowed funds* as it depends on the real rate of interest. Now consider a slightly different example. Suppose the $5000 inheritance is received now and the problem is to decide whether to buy the car now or in one year. If the car is bought later, the $5000 can be invested now and can earn interest for a year. Suppose that at a zero rate of inflation you can earn three percent in a savings account. Then in one year you will have $150 of interest earnings and it will still cost you the same amount, $5000, for the car. But in the event of five percent inflation that $150 of interest will not even cover the increased price of the car, the price increase of $250. If, with zero inflation, you had been indifferent between buying the car now and buying the car later when the interest earned is three percent, then you will again be indifferent during an inflationary period if the rate of interest on the savings account has increased by the same amount as the expected rate of inflation. With five percent inflation the savings account would have to earn an eight percent nominal rate of interest, the three percent real plus the five percent expected rate of inflation. Here, it is clear that the *supply of lendable funds* also depends on the real rate of interest.

Thus, in the long run, with a fully anticipated inflation of X percent per year, the nominal rate of interest will be bid up by X percentage points. Borrowers will be willing to pay the higher nominal rate of interest and lenders will demand the higher nominal rate of interest. We in fact observe that countries with high rates of inflation do indeed have high nominal rates of interest and countries with low rates of inflation have relatively low nominal rates of interest. The same is true of a given country at different points in time: when a country has a low rate of inflation it typically has a low nominal rate of interest and vice versa.

The relationship between real and nominal rates for the United States from 1948 through 1976 is shown in Fig. 5.3. In the figure the solid line is the nominal interest rate, represented by the monthly average three-month United States Treasury bill rate for the middle month of each calendar quarter.[2] The points in the figure show the realized real rate of interest on Treasury bills, calculated by subtracting from the bill rate the rate of increase in the Consumer Price Index over the life of the bill.[3] Somewhat surprisingly, the available evidence indicates that the real rate of interest on Treasury bills in the United States since the Korean War has averaged only one to two percent per annum.[4]

Figure 5.3 shows that the higher average level of the nominal interest rate after 1965 was not associated with a higher real rate of interest; in fact, the average real rate for the 1966–1976 period was clearly lower than for the 1955–1965 period. Thus, the higher rates of inflation after 1965 were not associated with commensurately higher nominal rates of interest.

While it is necessary to be cautious in generalizing from the particular case of a higher sustained inflation after 1965, this experience suggests either that a higher rate of inflation reduces the real rate of interest, or that the adjustment to inflation is slow and was far from complete even toward the end of the 1966–1976 period. The latter possibility seems especially likely

---

2   The bill rate plotted in Fig. 5.3 is not quite the same as the rate that appears in government statistics, shown in Fig. 5.1. That rate reflects the market convention of calculating the rate as

$$i = \frac{360}{n} (100 - P_B),$$

where P_B is the price per \$100 of maturity value of a bill with n days to maturity and i is in percent per annum. As can be seen from this formula, the market convention defines the interest rate as if a year had 360 days and as if the amount invested were \$100. To construct Fig. 5.3, the market quotes were adjusted to reflect the facts that a year actually has 365 days and that the amount actually invested is P_B.

3   Actually, the exact expression for the real rate of interest was used:

$$r = (i - \Delta P / P)/(1 + \Delta P / P).$$

4   See Fama 1975.

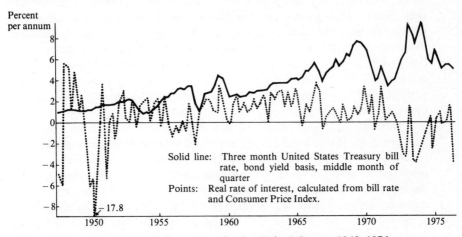

Fig. 5.3 Nominal and real interest rates in the United States, 1948–1976.

since the period contained three significant accelerations of inflation (in 1965–1966, 1968–1969, and in 1973–1974) that clearly caught people by surprise. In any event, it is clear that over a substantial period of time changes in the nominal rate of interest largely reflect changes in the rate of inflation.

Over short periods of time, however, people ordinarily do not realize what is happening to the rate of inflation, a point that was emphasized in discussing inflation in earlier chapters. It takes time before households and firms understand that the situation has changed and that a previous condition of relative stability in the rate of inflation has ended. As discussed in Chapter 4, when the rate of inflation initially rises and before inflationary expectations develop, business activity is generally strong. With unemployment low, households are borrowing funds to finance new cars, new homes, and so forth, and business firms are borrowing funds to finance the construction of new facilities. Because of these increased demands for funds, interest rates rise. But as the business expansion proceeds, wages and prices come under upward pressure, and the inflation rate begins to rise.

Because a reliable measure of inflationary expectations is not available, it is not possible unambiguously to divide a nominal interest rate change into components reflecting changes in the anticipated real rate and in the anticipated rate of inflation, and so it is not known how much of a nominal interest rate increase at the onset of inflation reflects inflationary anticipations and how much reflects the strong credit demands typical of a period of rising economic activity. What can be learned from examining Fig. 5.3, however, is that in the short run interest rate changes have often been in the correct direction but of insufficient magnitude to stabilize the realized real rate given the inflation rate that actually occurred. The nominal rate is moving in the correct direction, but by an insufficient amount, whenever nominal and real rates move in opposite directions. For some examples of this pattern, note that falling real rates were associated with rising nominal rates in 1956–1957, 1965–1966, and 1972–1973. For examples of the opposite pattern, note that rising real rates were associated with rising nominal rates in 1958 and, on average, from 1961 to 1964.

These observations justify an important general conclusion: No inference about the direction of change of the real interest rate can be drawn from an observed change in the nominal rate per se. Recent experience provides particularly dramatic evidence on this point. The realized real rate fell sharply from February 1972 to May 1973 even though the nominal rate on Treasury bills rose from 3.27 percent to 6.55 percent. And from mid-1974 to early 1975 the real rate rose even though the nominal rate fell sharply from 9.29 percent in August 1974 to 5.65 percent in February 1975. The true cost of borrowing, the real rate of interest, is most decidedly not measured, either in theory or in fact, by the nominal rate of interest.

It seems likely that in the short run a major part of an increased inflation is typically unanticipated, and so there is a wealth transfer from creditors to debtors. The wealth transfer occurs because people who had lent money expecting to receive, say, a two percent real rate of interest in fact receive a real rate of interest lower than anticipated. At the same time, of course, this lower real rate of interest is an unexpected bargain for those who have borrowed.

Expectations of inflation develop, however, as people observe the continuing inflation. And as these expectations develop, interest rates on new loans will adjust. But many long-term bonds, issued at the earlier rates, are still outstanding. As emphasized before, these bonds have fixed coupons that do not adjust as interest rates change. Therefore, as inflationary expectations rise, the prices of outstanding bonds are bid down. Thus this period is an especially painful one for bondholders. Not only are their fixed bond coupons worth less and less over time as the price level rises but also the market value of their bonds drops sharply. High quality long-term corporate bonds originally sold in the early 1960s with coupons about five percent were selling at only 60 to 70 percent of face value by the early 1970s.

THE BUSINESS CYCLE PATTERN OF INTEREST RATES

This discussion has emphasized that there are two principal factors over the business cycle that affect interest rates. One is the development of inflationary expectations and the other is the change in the demand for funds in order to finance business and consumer spending. Rising inflationary expectations generally accompany a business cycle expansion because as business booms, prices tend to rise and individuals come to believe that price increases will continue. Conversely, as business activity recedes, the rate of inflation generally falls and people come to realize that the weak markets do not afford a good opportunity to put through the same prices increases as before.

The effects of demands for durable goods were alluded to earlier and may now be discussed somewhat more fully. Much business and household spending is obviously financed by borrowing. Business firms float long-term bonds, and they borrow short term as well, in order to finance purchases of equipment, factory buildings, inventories, and so forth. Similarly, households borrow funds to finance purchases of houses, cars, TV sets, and so forth. When the economy moves into a recession and incomes fall, households reduce their purchases of these goods as they find themselves squeezed because of periods of unemployment, and business firms find that the demand for their output has fallen and therefore they have less need to expand their plants and equipment. For both reasons the demands for funds fall and therefore interest rates fall.

We may now tie together the effects of changes in the money stock on interest rates. When money growth first expands it tends to generate a business boom, as discussed in Chapter 4, and this boom adds to demand for borrowed funds by households and business firms. By the same token the business expansion tends to increase prices as people bid for goods; this process, if continued long enough, will degenerate into an ongoing inflation. As the inflation comes to be anticipated investors will demand higher nominal interest rates and borrowers will be willing to pay the higher interest rates. Money affects interest rates, therefore, because money affects both business activity and the rate of inflation.

In addition to the effects discussed above, money growth has a direct temporary impact on interest rates, though this impact is relatively unimportant quantitatively. Suppose the economy is fully adjusted to a particular rate of growth of money. Now assume that money growth suddenly rises. The higher money growth initially appears as an extra supply of loanable funds, and interest rates may tend to fall a bit. Of course, once the extra money growth begins to stimulate business activity, and later on inflation and inflationary expectations, interest rates will rise.

The tendency of higher money growth temporarily to depress interest rates temporarily is limited, and perhaps eliminated, by market anticipations of the eventual implications of higher money growth. If bond market participants expect the higher money growth to continue, they know that interest rates will shortly be higher and bond prices lower. No one wants to buy bonds when bond prices are expected to fall. Thus, higher money growth may immediately *depress* bond prices (raise interest rates) to the level expected to be implied in the future by the monetary policy being followed.

SUMMARY OF MONETARY EFFECTS ON INTEREST RATES

We may summarize the basic argument as follows: First, an increase in money growth tends to cause business to expand; the higher demand for cars, TV sets, factories, and so forth, adds to the demand for borrowed funds and raises interest rates. Second, the higher rate of money growth tends to raise the rate of inflation and inflationary anticipations, and the level of nominal interest rates is bid up accordingly. Third, in the very short run the process may go somewhat the other way. When the money stock is expanded, an extra supply of loanable funds is introduced into the credit markets and interest rates may fall temporarily.

If this very short-run effect is to operate, however, it must be that investors do not fully understand what is happening. If investors see the central bank buying large amounts of securities and believe that an inflationary monetary expansion will ensue, then they will not be eager to hold onto their bonds at higher prices. Therefore the very short-run effect of money on interest rates can occur only to the extent that investors do not realize that money growth is expanding, do not fully understand the implications of a higher rate of money growth, or believe that the extra money creation is temporary and will be reversed. Especially given the experience of recent years, the inflationary implications of excessive money growth probably are understood by most investors; however, it is quite difficult to figure out exactly when a higher rate of money growth is a temporary phenomenon and when it is a more permanent feature of central bank policy.

This point is an extremely important one. Interest rates, and indeed many other aspects of economic behavior, will depend in part on the interpretation that people give to the actions of the monetary authorities and of government policymakers in general. Thus whatever may be predicted under the assumption that people's expectations have not changed, the prediction must be regarded warily because expectations cannot be assumed to be independent of policy actions. Expectations of inflation are not formed only from looking at the past rate of inflation; anyone who is attempting to get one step ahead of the game will not wait for the inflation to develop but will look directly at the underlying causes of inflation. For this reason, in assessing the impact of changes in the money stock on interest rates and other variables, it is always extremely important to take into account the way in which the monetary changes affect the expectations of households and business firms.

REFERENCE

Fama, Eugene F., 1975. Short-term interest rates as predictors of inflation, *American Economic Review* **65** (June): 269–282.

The Creation 6
and Destruction
of Money

This chapter outlines the main features of the system by which the money stock is determined. The institutional system in the United States—the commercial banks, other financial institutions, the central bank, and the United States Treasury—is quite a complicated one but we will discuss only the main features of the system as required for the chapter on monetary policy that follows. Although the discussion is confined to the United States monetary system, the basic principles examined apply to foreign monetary systems as well even though those systems differ in many important respects from the United States system.

COMMERCIAL BANKS

The deposit component of the money stock is far larger than the currency component, and the deposit component has historically fluctuated much more than the currency component. Bank deposits, both demand and time (or savings) deposits, are liabilities of the banks, funds owed by the banks to the depositors. To understand why deposits fluctuate, an examination of bank balance sheets is required. The balance sheet is a statement of a firm's asset and liability position as of a particular time, such as the close of business on the last day of the month.

The balance sheet of the individual commercial bank has as its principal assets reserves (funds held on deposit at Federal Reserve Banks and currency and coin held in banks' vaults) loans to households and business firms, and investments in bills, bonds, notes, and mortgages of various kinds. The principal liabilities are deposits of various kinds and loans from the central bank. It can be seen from Table 6.1 (reproduced from the Federal Reserve Bulletin) that these items do in fact include the major part of the dollar value of banks' assets and liabilities.

Table 6.1   Commercial bank assets and liabilities · Detailed balance sheet, December 31, 1976 · Asset and liability items are shown in millions of dollars.

Asset account	All commercial banks	Insured commercial banks	Member banks[1] Total	New York City	City of Chicago	Other large	All other	Non-member banks[1]
1 Cash bank balances, items in process	136,075	129,578	108,934	29,494	3,934	40,471	35,034	27,141
2 Currency and coin	12,124	12,115	9,066	332	220	3,048	4,965	3,059
3 Reserves with F.R. Banks	25,968	25,968	25,968	3,585	1,423	10,627	10,334	
4 Demand balances with banks in United States	36,815	32,964	19,711	7,389	196	3,324	8,804	17,103
5 Other balances with banks in United States	6,972	5,763	3,623	193	34	1,434	1,961	3,349
6 Balances with banks in foreign countries	5,823	4,509	4,046	836	23	2,102	1,085	1,777
7 Cash items in process of collection	48,374	48,260	46,520	16,659	2,038	19,937	7,886	1,854
8 Total securities held—Book value	249,882	247,439	176,333	21,349	8,157	57,755	89,072	73,549
9 U.S. Treasury	102,514	101,460	74,577	11,823	4,072	25,735	32,948	27,937
10 Other U.S. Govt. agencies	35,838	35,460	22,150	1,355	500	6,237	14,059	13,688
11 States and political subdivisions	104,661	104,374	75,310	7,751	3,349	24,546	39,665	29,330
12 All other securities	6,732	6,220	4,217	421	236	1,191	2,370	2,515
13 Unclassified total	137	137	78			47	30	60
14 *Trading-account securities*	7,904	7,882	7,650	3,251	832	3,246	322	253
15 U.S. Treasury	5,011	5,011	4,861	2,386	582	1,705	188	151
16 Other U.S. Govt. agencies	991	991	975	259	55	624	38	15
17 States and political subdivisions	1,324	1,324	1,297	479	110	660	48	27
18 All other trading acct. securities	440	440	440	127	86	209	17	
19 Unclassified	137	116	78			47	30	60
20 *Bank investment portfolios*	241,979	239,557	168,683	18,098	7,325	54,510	88,750	73,296
21 U.S. Treasury	97,503	96,449	69,717	9,437	3,490	24,030	32,760	27,786
22 Other U.S. Govt. agencies	34,847	34,279	21,175	1,096	445	5,613	14,021	13,672
23 States and political subdivisions	103,336	103,049	74,013	7,272	3,239	23,885	39,617	29,323
24 All other portfolio securities	6,292	5,780	3,778	293	151	981	2,352	2,515
25 F.R. stock and corporate stock	1,580	1,541	1,313	281	86	497	449	268
26 Federal funds sold and securities resale agreement	48,346	45,767	36,378	1,993	1,339	19,648	13,398	11,968
27 Commercial banks	40,199	37,876	28,780	979	1,035	14,217	12,550	11,419
28 Brokers and dealers	5,775	5,693	5,499	610	192	3,981	716	275
29 Others	2,373	2,198	2,099	404	113	1,450	132	273
30 Other loans, gross	546,704	532,945	406,579	75,468	21,807	148,516	160,788	140,124
31 LESS: Unearned income on loans	12,577	12,526	8,614	561	82	2,856	5,117	3,963
32 Reserves for loan loss	6,192	6,116	4,899	1,185	300	1,751	1,663	1,293
33 Other loans, net	527,934	514,303	393,066	73,722	21,426	143,909	154,008	134,869

Other loans, gross, by category

#	Item								
34	*Real estate loans*	149,483	149,276	104,774	9,419	1,848	37,462	55,984	44,769
35	Construction and land development	16,644	16,638	13,153	2,801	382	6,039	3,931	3,491
36	Secured by farmland	6,721	6,710	2,868	16	14	295	2,543	3,853
37	Secured by residential	84,922	84,784	60,487	4,433	944	21,816	33,294	24,435
38	1- to 4-family residences	80,394	80,265	57,201	3,992	845	20,639	31,726	23,193
39	FHA-insured or VA-guaranteed	7,956	7,919	6,859	381	49	3,670	2,529	1,097
40	Conventional	72,438	72,346	50,342	3,611	797	16,968	29,196	22,096
41	Multifamily residences	4,528	4,519	3,286	447	99	1,178	1,568	1,241
42	FHA-insured	388	387	323	122	25	95	82	64
43	Conventional	4,140	4,132	2,963	320	74	1,083	1,486	1,177
44	Secured by other properties	41,195	41,144	28,206	2,169	509	9,311	16,216	12,989
45	*Loans to financial institutions*	42,427	35,738	33,760	12,048	4,383	14,349	2,981	8,666
46	To REIT's and mortgage companies	9,982	9,855	9,515	3,496	1,301	4,045	674	2,335
47	To domestic commercial banks	4,531	2,774	2,196	3,606	127	1,126	337	4,393
48	To banks in foreign countries	10,880	6,617	6,487	3,022	290	2,717	457	309
49	To other depository institutions	1,482	1,340	1,173	163	24	789	198	1,164
50	To other financial institutions	15,552	15,151	14,389	1,761	2,641	5,672	1,315	465
51	Loans to security brokers and dealers	11,420	11,075	10,793	6,900	1,417	2,267	209	627
52	Other loans to purch./carry securities	4,032	4,015	3,329	336	317	1,701	975	703
53	Loans to farmers—except real estate	23,282	23,259	12,971	128	149	3,028	9,667	10,311
54	Commercial and industrial loans	182,920	177,028	145,849	37,893	11,018	55,108	41,830	37,071
55	Loans to individuals	118,408	118,051	82,896	6,003	1,820	29,066	46,005	35,512
56	*Instalment loans*	94,078	93,751	65,619	4,428	1,040	23,385	36,766	28,458
57	Passenger automobiles	39,862	39,588	25,641	790	136	7,397	17,318	14,221
58	Residential-repair/modernize	6,523	6,522	4,589	324	55	1,808	3,422	1,933
59	Credit cards and related plans	14,358	14,353	12,675	1,649	669	6,935	2,618	1,683
60	Charge-account credit cards	11,317	11,317	10,172	1,186	637	5,731	803	1,146
61	Check and revolving credit plans	3,041	3,036	2,504	463	33	1,205	1,815	537
62	Other retail consumer goods	15,937	15,930	10,974	327	73	3,886	6,689	4,963
63	Mobile homes	8,743	8,742	6,217	173	28	2,231	3,785	2,525
64	Other	7,195	7,189	4,757	154	44	1,654	2,904	2,438
65	Other instalment loans	17,397	17,358	11,739	1,338	106	3,360	6,935	5,658
66	Single-payment loans to individuals	24,330	24,300	17,276	1,575	781	5,681	9,239	7,054
67	All other loans	14,732	14,405	12,267	2,741	855	5,533	3,137	2,466
68	Total loans and securities, net	827,742	809,050	607,089	97,344	31,009	221,810	256,927	220,653
69	Direct lease financing	5,111	5,111	4,865	1,088	129	2,910	738	246
70	Fixed assets—Buildings, furniture, real estate	19,539	19,448	14,616	1,949	662	5,680	6,325	4,923
71	Investment in unconsolidated subsidiaries	2,341	2,303	2,272	1,000	206	978	89	68
72	Customer acceptances outstanding	9,505	9,147	8,758	4,125	177	4,169	288	747
73	Other assets	30,498	29,384	26,355	9,322	1,651	11,257	4,126	4,142
74	Total assets	1,030,811	1,004,020	772,890	144,323	37,767	287,274	303,526	257,922

For notes see opposite page.

Liability or capital account	All commercial banks	Insured commercial banks	Member banks[1]					Non-member banks[1]
			Total	Large banks			All other	
				New York City	City of Chicago	Other large		
75 Demand deposits	336,800	332,283	260,090	60,201	10,267	92,746	96,876	76,711
76 Mutual savings banks	1,684	1,385	1,254	624	2	268	360	430
77 Other individuals, partnerships, and corporations	255,433	254,221	192,616	32,600	7,552	72,262	80,201	62,818
78 U.S. Govt.	3,025	3,020	2,103	134	41	669	1,259	921
79 States and political subdivisions	17,715	17,648	12,071	645	125	3,568	7,733	5,644
80 Foreign governments, central banks, etc.	2,414	1,846	1,813	1,365	35	387	26	601
81 Commercial banks in United States	36,256	35,926	34,679	16,412	2,022	11,852	4,394	1,577
82 Banks in foreign countries	7,410	6,761	6,512	5,345	174	862	4,132	898
83 Certified and officers checks, etc.	12,864	11,475	9,041	3,076	318	2,878	2,769	3,822
84 Time deposits	298,276	289,949	212,936	33,842	12,151	73,759	93,183	85,340
85 Accumulated for personal loan payments	146	146	118	145	6	10	108	28
86 Mutual savings banks	339	317	296			125	20	43
87 Other individuals, partnerships, and corporations	233,964	228,522	166,393	25,005	8,745	56,289	76,354	67,571
88 U.S. Govt.	675	675	514	66	27	205	216	161
89 States and political subdivisions	44,165	43,885	30,407	1,203	861	12,835	15,508	13,758
90 Foreign governments, central banks, etc.	10,044	8,481	8,218	4,574	1,408	2,185	52	1,827
91 Commercial banks in United States	7,139	6,709	5,858	2,148	1,011	1,878	820	1,281
92 Banks in foreign countries	1,803	1,213	1,132	702	94	231	106	670
93 Savings deposits	203,251	202,770	145,835	11,157	2,983	54,407	77,288	57,416
94 Individuals and nonprofit organizations	188,391	187,922	134,596	10,209	2,782	49,570	72,036	53,795
95 Corporations and other profit organizations	8,642	8,633	6,420	480	175	2,761	3,003	2,222
96 U.S. Govt.	6,103	6,100	4,719	388	25	2,060	2,245	1,384
97 All other	115	115	100	79		16	4	15
98 Total deposits	838,328	825,002	618,860	105,200	25,401	220,912	267,347	219,468
99 Federal funds purchased and securities sold under agreements to repurchase	72,847	70,188	66,899	15,000	8,643	34,537	8,719	5,948
100 Commercial banks	42,819	40,613	39,195	6,523	7,241	20,844	4,587	3,624
101 Brokers and dealers	5,603	5,577	5,345	949	29	3,651	716	258
102 Others	24,425	23,998	22,360	7,529	1,373	10,041	3,416	2,066
103 Other liabilities for borrowed money	7,304	5,120	4,840	2,500	49	1,919	372	2,464
104 Mortgage indebtedness	776	774	548	66	15	271	196	227
105 Bank acceptances outstanding	10,118	9,755	9,366	4,714	177	4,186	288	752
106 Other liabilities	23,389	16,013	13,772	4,539	805	5,298	3,129	9,617
107 Total liabilities	952,761	926,852	714,285	132,020	35,091	267,122	280,052	238,476

108 Subordinated notes and debentures	1,079	1,053	1,823	83	1,124	4,082	5,098	5,161
109 **Equity capital**	**18,366**	**22,421**	**18,329**	**2,593**	**11,179**	**54,522**	**72,070**	**72,889**
110 Preferred stock	48	23	2			25	67	73
111 Common stock	4,356	5,041	3,818	570	2,453	11,882	16,143	16,238
112 Surplus	7,798	8,280	7,655	1,243	4,229	21,407	28,791	29,205
113 Undivided profits	5,575	8,373	6,422	728	4,406	19,929	25,266	25,505
114 Other capital reserves	589	705	432	52	91	1,279	1,803	1,868
115 **Total liabilities and equity capital**	**257,922**	**303,526**	**287,274**	**37,767**	**144,323**	**772,890**	**1,004,020**	**1,030,811**
MEMO ITEMS:								
116 Demand deposits adjusted[2]	72,359	83,336	60,288	6,167	26,996	176,787	245,076	249,146
Average for last 15 or 30 days:								
117 Cash and due from bank	22,936	33,154	39,824	4,372	29,510	106,860	125,226	129,797
118 Federal funds sold and securities purchased under agreements to resell	13,420	13,883	17,825	1,425	2,307	35,440	45,794	48,860
119 Total loans	135,064	154,831	143,957	21,349	73,976	394,113	515,977	529,177
120 Time deposits of $100,000 or more	29,736	28,073	43,372	9,682	28,517	109,644	132,893	139,381
121 Total deposits	215,693	263,259	213,361	24,869	98,932	600,420	803,019	816,113
122 Federal funds purchased and securities sold under agreements to repurchase	5,458	9,135	35,775	9,340	20,453	74,703	77,949	80,161
123 Other liabilities for borrowed money	2,540	335	1,842	53	2,165	4,396	4,686	6,936
124 Standby letters of credit outstanding	2,153	762	3,162	921	6,494	11,340	12,969	13,493
125 Time deposits of $100,000 or more	29,738	28,492	44,546	9,582	28,795	111,415	135,031	141,153
126 Certificates of deposit	24,368	24,285	35,878	8,276	24,451	92,891	113,275	117,258
127 Other time deposits	5,371	4,207	8,668	1,306	4,344	18,524	21,756	23,895
128 Number of banks	8,914	5,583	154	9	12	5,758	14,397	14,672

▲ Data for insured commercial banks for Sept. 30, 1976, appear on pp. A-70 and A-71.

[1] Member banks exclude and nonmember banks include 8 noninsured trust companies that are members of the Federal Reserve System, and member banks exclude 2 national banks outside the continental United States.

[2] Demand deposits adjusted are demand deposits other than domestic commercial interbank and U.S. Govt., less cash items reported as in process of collection.

NOTE.—Data include consolidated reports, including figures for all bank-premises subsidiaries and other significant majority-owned domestic subsidiaries. Securities are reported on a gross basis before deductions of valuation reserves. Holdings by type of security will be reported as soon as they become available.

Back data in lesser detail were shown in previous BULLETINS. Details may not add to totals because of rounding.

To understand how the total amount of deposits may change from one point in time to another, consider first the situation faced by an individual bank. Suppose that the bank is required by law to hold reserves equal to 20 percent of its deposits, and for simplicity suppose that only demand deposits are considered. Now let a person bring a $100 check to Bank A and deposit it in a demand deposit account. The bank takes the check to a Federal Reserve Bank for collection: the bank ends up with an additional $100 in reserve balances and the individual ends up with an additional $100 in a demand deposit account. Since deposits have gone up by $100, the bank's required reserves have gone up by $20. But since the bank's total reserves have gone up by $100, the bank now has excess reserves of $80.

The bank could simply hold the excess reserves, but it has a powerful incentive not to do so. Reserve balances earn no interest. If the bank lends out the $80 in excess reserves, it will be able to earn interest and to increase its earnings for the year. So, let us suppose that the bank does in fact make use of the $80 of excess reserves by accepting a loan application. The borrower takes the funds and uses them to buy some good, perhaps a component for a stereo system, and so the seller of the good now has the $80. What does the seller of the good do with the $80? In general the seller will take the $80 and deposit the funds in a bank, perhaps the same bank that provided the original loan but probably a different bank, Bank B.

Now it can be seen that Bank A no longer has excess reserves but that Bank B has an increase in deposits of $80 and an increase in reserves of $80. The $80 check that has been deposited in Bank B has exactly the same type of effect as the original $100 check deposited in Bank A. Bank B has an increase in required reserves of 20 percent of the $80, or $16. Thus, Bank B now has excess reserves of $64. And so the process can continue with additional loans and additional deposits until all the excess reserves are used up.

What level of deposits will use up the excess reserves? If we assume that the initial $100 deposit came, so to speak, out of nowhere, and if we assume that all funds lent out are spent and redeposited, then deposits in the banking system as a whole must rise by $500 to absorb all of the original reserve increase of $100. A 20 percent reserve requirement on $500 of deposits is $100 in required reserves, just absorbing the $100 increase in reserves.

But before we conclude that the original $100 deposit increases reserves by $100 and total deposits by $500 we must return to ask the question about where that $100 came from in the first place. Checks do not come, "so to speak, out of nowhere." Clearly, if the $100 came from a check written on Bank C, then Bank C suffers a deposit and reserve outflow when the check clears and will find itself in a position of *deficient* reserves. Recall that Bank A had sent the check to a Federal Reserve Bank for collection. The Federal Reserve collects the check for Bank A by adding $100 to Bank A's reserve account and subtracting $100 from Bank C's reserve account. The Fed also sends the check back to Bank C which then reduces the account upon which the check was written and sends the cancelled check back to the person who wrote it.

The deficient reserve position of Bank C exactly offsets the excess reserve position of Bank A. Thus, at the same time that the deposit expansion process sketched above was going on, a deposit contraction process must also be going on. When Bank C found itself with its deposits down by $100 and its reserves down by $100, its required reserves were down by $20 leaving a reserve deficiency of $80. Bank C might respond, for example, by selling $80 in securities. But the securities are paid for by a check written on Bank D and, when that check clears, Bank D will be left with a reserve deficiency of $64. And so forth.

The deposit expansion–contraction process is of great practical significance, but another process also needs to be understood. Suppose Bank A in the example above thought that the $100 inflow was likely to be reversed in the near future. If Bank A expanded its loans and then later suffered a $100 outflow, it would have to contract as Bank C did in our example. Instead of lending $80 to the person buying stereo equipment, Bank A might lend the $80 to another bank. Similarly, if Bank C thought that its $100 reserve drain was likely to be temporary, it might not want to sell securities. Instead, Bank C might borrow $80 in reserves from another bank such as Bank A that has temporary surplus funds.

The market in which banks borrow and lend reserves from each other is called the *federal funds market*. Federal funds are nothing more than reserve balances on deposit at Federal Reserve Banks. In the federal funds market, loans are generally made for one day—"overnight" in market terminology. In our example, Bank C might borrow $80 in federal funds from Bank A; if the deposit flows are not reversed in one day, Bank C may borrow again the next day. If the deposit flows are not reversed, the banks will in time consider the flows permanent rather than temporary and undertake loan expansion or contraction as described earlier.

From this discussion it should be clear that for total deposits to increase (decrease) it is necessary that there be an inflow (outflow) of reserves to the banking system as a whole. No expansion for the system as a whole can take place through the *transfer* of deposits and reserves from one bank to another.

How, then, can the banking system as a whole receive an inflow of reserves? One way is for the first bank to receive a deposit of currency rather than a check drawn on another bank. If the currency comes from someone's pocket, then no other bank has suffered a withdrawal but the first bank has found itself with a deposit and reserve increase. In this case the deposit expansion outlined earlier can continue without being offset by a contraction process through a different series of banks. The net result would be that deposits will have gone up by $500 and currency in circulation outside the banking system will have gone down by $100, so that the money stock, deposits plus currency in circulation outside the banking system, will have increased a net of $400.

This example shows that the money creation and destruction process has as one important component the extent to which the general public holds currency as opposed to holding deposits. When the public decides to hold more deposits and less currency, the net result is for the *sum* of the two to rise, all other things equal. Conversely, if the public decides to hold more currency and fewer deposits, the sum of the two falls.

THE CENTRAL BANK

In the discussion above it was noted that the commercial banks hold some of their reserves in the form of deposits at the central bank. Changes in these reserves, if not offset by currency reserves held in the banks' vaults, will change the amount of deposits, assuming the required reserve ratio (20 percent in our examples) remains unchanged. To understand how these reserve balances can change, we must examine the central bank's balance sheet.

The balance sheet of the central bank, the Federal Reserve System in the United States, has the following major items. On the asset side the major items are gold certificates and international reserve items, government securities, and loans to banks. On the liability side the major items are notes (currency) outstanding, and balances due commercial banks (their reserves), the United States Treasury, and foreign governments and central banks. The balance sheet for the Federal Reserve System is shown in Table 6.2.

It is important to understand the meaning of the "liabilities" listed by the central bank. The liabilities are of two very different kinds. On the one hand, there are liabilities consisting of debts owed by the central bank to its own employees, suppliers, and so forth, reported on line 31 of Table 6.2. These liabilities are of exactly the same kind as the liabilities of any business firm or bank. But the bulk of the central bank's liabilities consist of currency outstanding (Federal Reserve "notes" in the United States) and the reserve balances of the commercial banks. These liabilities are very different from the usual liabilities of business firms.

The difference between the two types of liabilities can be seen as follows. Suppose a supplier of paper and pencils to the central bank calls up and complains that the bill for these items has not been paid. Clearly, the central bank owes the supplier for the items purchased and should be expected to pay up promptly. Now suppose that you take a Federal Reserve note, perhaps a ten-dollar bill, to the central bank and ask it to "pay up." How will the central bank pay you? You might receive two five-dollar bills, or ten ones, or five twos, or a hundred dimes. You will not receive anything that is much different from what you already had. It is clear that *these* central bank liabilities are not like the liabilities that business firms have. Currency is an *asset* for a business firm, and can be used to pay off a liability, such as an overdue bill. Currency is listed as a liability on the central bank's balance sheet only as a result of a misleading accounting convention dating from the time when currency really was a liability: it used to be the case that the central bank was required by law to pay off (directly or indirectly) its currency liabilities in gold, an item appearing on the asset side of the central bank's balance sheet.

Another approach to understanding the nonliability nature of the central bank's reserve and currency "liabilities" is to explore what happens when the central bank exercises its power to purchase government bonds. How are these bonds paid for? The central bank writes a check *on itself* and gives the check to the person who sold the government bonds. The person who sold the bonds takes the check and deposits it in a demand deposit account at a commercial bank. The commercial bank takes the check back to the central bank for collection and the central bank "pays off" by increasing the commercial bank's reserve balance at the central bank. The reserve balance is a strange liability indeed. It is *created* by the central bank buying government bonds and once created there is nothing that the owner of the "liability," the bank owning the reserve balance in this example, can collect other than another reserve balance or Federal Reserve notes.

This example should make clear that the central bank can quite literally create money. The central bank creates money every bit as easily as the counterfeiter creates money. All it takes is a roll of the printing press, or of the accountant's pen making a bookkeeping entry, or of the accountant's instruction making a computerized bookkeeping entry. The only difference is that printing money is legal for the central bank but not for the counterfeiter. Clearly, the power to create money by rolling the presses is tremendously important. Rolling the presses to create money is not a right that can be given to every citizen.[1] And when that right is given to the central bank, the power to create money must be used with the greatest responsibility.

So now let us suppose that the central bank has indeed purchased some government bonds and has created new banks reserves by doing so. This,

---

1   Actually this statement is subject to considerable dispute. Private creation of currency in the form of banknotes was common in the United States in the 19th century. To stay in business a bank had an interest in ensuring that its notes, which bore the bank's name, were issued in reasonable amounts and were redeemed in gold by the bank on demand. While many people suffered losses when bank notes issued by particular banks became worthless after the banks failed, many have also suffered losses when the value of national currencies was destroyed by overissue and generalized inflation. Whatever may be the relative merits of currency systems relying on privately issued and governmentally issued currency, what is clear is that governments ought not to permit counterfeiting per se, the printing of currency with someone else's name on the currency.

Table 6.2 Federal reserve banks. Condition and F.R. note statements in millions of dollars.

	Account	Wednesday 1976					End of month 1976		
		Dec. 1	Dec. 8	Dec. 15	Dec. 22p	Dec. 29p	Oct. 31	Nov. 30	Dec. 31p
		Consolidated condition statement							
	ASSETS								
1	Gold certificate account	11,598	11,598	11,598	11,598	11,598	11,598	11,598	11,598
2	Special Drawing Rights certificate account	1,200	1,200	1,200	1,200	1,200	1,200	1,200	1,200
3	Cash	357	356	358	361	357	381	362	364
	Loans:								
4	Member bank borrowings	349	24	329	75	375	44	40	26
5	Other								
	Acceptances:								
6	Bought outright	197	189	195	195	196	197	188	196
7	Held under repurchase agreements			349	513	821	140		795
	Federal agency obligations:								
8	Bought outright	6,833	6,833	6,794	6,794	6,794	6,757	6,857	6,794
9	Held under repurchase agreements			100	218	409	79		278
	U.S. Govt. securities:								
	Bought outright:								
10	Bills	35,867	37,944	37,711	37,527	37,345	39,875	37,992	38,571
11	Certificates—Special								
12	Other								
13	Notes	47,089	47,089	47,089	47,470	47,470	46,897	47,089	47,972
14	Bonds	6,579	6,579	6,579	6,690	6,690	6,506	6,579	6,725
15	Total[1]	89,535	91,612	91,379	91,687	91,505	93,278	91,660	93,268
16	Held under repurchase agreements			2,934	6,475	9,454	2,561		3,753
17	Total U.S. Govt. securities	89,535	91,612	94,313	98,162	100,959	95,839	91,660	97,021
18	Total loans and securities	96,914	98,658	102,080	105,957	109,554	103,056	98,745	105,110
19	Cash items in process of collection	9,765	8,717	10,471	11,260	8,644	6,731	8,785	7,735
20	Bank premises	364	366	366	367	363	358	364	363
21	Operating equipment	28	27	27	26	26	26	28	25
	Other assets:								
22	Denominated in foreign currencies	544	545	241	183	175	401	546	170
23	All other	2,702	2,385	2,526	2,542	2,678	2,985	2,423	2,624
24	Total assets	123,472	123,852	128,867	133,494	134,595	126,736	124,051	129,189

LIABILITIES

25 F.R. notes	83,068	83,613	84,034	84,477	84,494	80,389	83,055	83,731
Deposits:								
26 Member bank reserves	23,567	27,834	30,770	29,352	30,031	26,461	23,239	25,059
27 U.S. Treasury—General account	6,189	3,011	3,328	8,632	9,684	10,238	6,766	10,393
28 Foreign	312	292	335	287	257	362	305	352
29 Other²	1,176	970	885	840	932	953	1,022	1,357
30 Total deposits	31,244	32,107	35,318	39,111	40,904	38,014	31,332	37,161
31 Deferred availability cash items	5,672	5,107	6,296	6,539	5,630	4,718	6,150	5,234
32 Other liabilities and accrued dividends	1,026	942	1,023	1,056	1,152	1,165	1,065	1,097
33 Total liabilities	121,010	121,769	126,671	131,183	132,180	124,286	121,602	127,223
CAPITAL ACCOUNTS								
34 Capital paid in	974	974	975	980	984	974	974	983
35 Surplus	929	929	929	929	929	929	929	983
36 Other capital accounts	559	180	292	402	502	547	546	
37 Total liabilities and capital accounts	123,472	123,852	128,867	133,494	134,595	126,736	124,051	129,189
38 MEMO: Marketable U.S. Govt. securities held in custody for foreign and intl. account	48,233	49,730	50,004	50,319	50,345	47,497	48,000	50,269
Federal Reserve note statement								
39 F.R. notes outstanding (issued to Bank)	87,682	87,997	88,486	89,035	89,262	85,907	87,650	89,303
Collateral held against notes outstanding:								
40 Gold certificate account	11,596	11,596	11,596	11,596	11,596	11,595	11,596	11,596
41 Special Drawing Rights certificate account	643	643	643	643	643	619	643	643
42 Acceptances								
43 U.S. Govt. securities	76,900	77,240	77,490	77,850	78,050	75,680	76,850	78,100
44 Total collateral	89,139	89,479	89,729	90,089	90,289	87,894	89,089	90,339

¹ *Includes* securities loaned—fully guaranteed by U.S. Govt. securities pledged with F.R. Banks—and *excludes* (if any) securities sold and scheduled to be bought back under matched sale-purchase transactions.

² Includes certain deposits of domestic nonmember banks and foreign-owned banking institutions voluntarily held with member banks and redeposited in full with F.R. Banks.

then, is another case in which a commercial bank receives a check and has an increase in its deposits and reserves. But in this case the check was not drawn on another commercial bank; it was a check drawn on a Federal Reserve Bank. Therefore, this increase in reserves does leave the banking system as a whole with excess reserves. The net result after the money creation process has run its course is for the level of deposits to rise by $500 given that the increase in reserves is $100, that the required reserve ratio is 20 percent, and that no currency drains occur.

One additional way in which bank reserves can change is through commercial banks borrowing from the central bank. If a commercial bank decides to borrow, and the central bank is willing to lend, the central bank writes up the commercial bank's reserve account at the central bank and writes up the central bank's asset account "loans to commercial banks." The commercial bank can then use the funds to buy securities or make loans to its customers, but in the process of doing so transfers the funds to other banks which then are able to use those funds as reserves. Unless offset by other factors, then, central bank loans to the commercial banks increase total reserves in the banking system and therefore increase the amount of deposits in the commercial banks.

To summarize the main point of this discussion, the *total* reserves of the commercial banking system are changed through the activities of the central bank. One mechanism is through central bank *open-market operations*—purchases and sales of government securities in the open market. A second way is through the extension and repayment of *central bank loans* to the commercial banks. Total reserves are also changed a third way, not directly involving the central bank, through the public changing the amount of currency it holds: when currency flows from general circulation into the commercial banks, the banks' reserves are increased and, conversely, when the public takes currency out of the commercial banks, the banks' reserves are decreased.

THE UNITED STATES TREASURY

One other important item on the central bank balance sheet deserves attention: deposits by the United States Treasury into the central bank. These are the deposits on which the Treasury writes checks to pay its bills. When the Treasury writes a check to pay a bill and the check is sent to a government supplier or employee, the effect is to increase bank reserves in the short run. The person who receives a government check deposits it in a demand deposit account at a commercial bank. The commercial bank then takes the check and asks the Federal Reserve to credit the bank's reserve account at the Federal Reserve. The Federal Reserve does so, taking the funds out of the United States Treasury's account at the Federal Reserve.

The Treasury, however, cannot write checks on its accounts at the Federal Reserve without having funds in those accounts. Money flows into those accounts as the Treasury collects taxes. How are taxes paid? Individuals and corporations send checks to the Treasury, checks drawn on deposit accounts at the commercial banks. The Treasury takes the checks and (directly or indirectly) deposits them in accounts at Federal Reserve Banks. The Federal Reserve then deducts the amounts written on the checks from the reserve balances held in the Federal Reserve Banks by the commercial banks upon which the checks were drawn and sends the checks back to the commercial banks. The individual banks receive the checks, take the funds out of depositors' accounts, and send the cancelled checks back to the depositors.

It can be seen, therefore, that if the Treasury's tax revenues match its expenditures, then there is no change in the total amount of money outstanding; there is simply a circuit of money from the taxpayer to the Treasury and then from the Treasury back into the banking system as suppliers and government employees are paid. As long as the Treasury's accounts at the Federal Reserve banks do not change (tax inflows match government expenditures) the Treasury operations will not affect the total amount of money in circulation.

The Treasury does not, however, always have tax revenues sufficient to pay all of its bills: the government may have a budget deficit. What does the Treasury do in this case? To cover a deficit the Treasury sells bonds and/or bills. Most of these bonds are sold to the general public. When people pay for Treasury bonds, they do so in the form of checks written on their deposit accounts at commercial banks. There is, therefore, a circuit of money from the public to the Treasury in the form of checks written to pay tax bills *and* to buy government bonds, and back to the public as the Treasury spends the funds to pay its expenses. Since the bonds sold to finance the deficit (or bonds retired when there is a budget surplus) match the difference between Treasury spending and tax revenues, the total amount of money coming into the Treasury matches the total amount going out leaving the amount held by the general public unchanged except for short-run and temporary fluctuations.

Treasury financing has been examined under the assumption that bonds are sold to the general public. Suppose instead that the Treasury sells bonds directly to the Federal Reserve System. What happens then? In this case the Treasury is taking in funds *not* received from the general public and then putting the funds into the hands of the general public when government bills are paid. The Federal Reserve purchase of the government bonds has the effect of increasing the reserves in the banking system and allowing monetary expansion. It can be seen, therefore, that government deficit spending can increase the quantity of money in the hands of the public *only* insofar as the central bank buys the government bonds sold to cover the deficit. As long as the central bank refuses to buy the bonds, there can be no monetary expansion as a result of the deficit spending.

THE MONETARY BASE

The major monetary "liabilities" of the Federal Reserve are Federal Reserve notes and bank reserves on deposit at Federal Reserve Banks. The sum of these two items is called the "monetary base" or, sometimes, "high-powered money." The significance of this concept is that a nation's money stock (currency in the hands of the general public plus commercial bank deposits) can be viewed as being built upon the monetary base.

Before proceeding with the analysis of the monetary base, a nuisance matter must be clarified. As mentioned earlier, some Federal Reserve notes are in the hands of the general public and some are in commercial bank vaults. The former make up the currency component of the money stock, and the latter the bank's vault cash. Total bank reserves consist of reserves on deposit at Federal Reserve Banks plus vault cash.[2] In analyzing the significance of the monetary base, it is convenient to lump together bank reserves on deposit at the Federal Reserve and bank vault cash reserves, and simply call the sum "reserves."

With this convention, we may treat the monetary base as having two components: bank reserves and currency in the hands of the public. Thus, we may write

$$H = R + C,$$

where the symbol H has been used for the monetary base instead of the symbol B in order to avoid possible confusion with the earlier use (in Chapter 3) of B for "bonds."

In discussing currency earlier in this chapter it was noted that the total money stock will tend to rise (fall) when currency is deposited in (withdrawn from) a bank, but there was no discussion to indicate why currency might flow into or out of banks. Suppose, now, that households and firms on the average want to hold a certain fraction, h, of their total holdings of money in the form of currency. In this case, the fraction $(1 - h)$ is held in the form of deposits, and we may write

$$C = hM$$

$$D = (1 - h)M.$$

---

2 Reserve requirement regulations with respect to vault cash have been changed from time to time. As of this writing banks are permitted to count all their vault cash as reserves but at various times in the past banks were not permitted to count vault cash as reserves, or were permitted to count only a fraction of their vault cash.

Last, from the discussion concerning reserve requirements we have

$$R = kD$$

where k is the reserve ratio (which was 0.2 in the examples discussed earlier). Now these separate components can be put together as follows:

$$H = R + C = kD + C = k(1 - h)M + hM.$$

Thus, we have

$$M = \frac{H}{k(1 - h) + h}.$$

This expression shows the relationship between the monetary base, the currency ratio, the reserve ratio, and the money stock.

Relating the money stock to the monetary base is useful in studying the major factors causing fluctuations in the money stock. For example, the large contraction in the money stock between 1929 and 1933 had as its proximate cause a large increase in the currency ratio, h. That increase, in turn, was a natural consequence of a long series of bank failures. Depositors, fearing for the safety of funds held in banks, withdrew their funds and held a larger fraction of their total money balances in currency. But as they withdrew funds, since the monetary base was roughly constant over this period, the total money stock fell.

The reserve ratio depends on both the required reserve ratio and the amount of excess reserves held by banks. Excess reserves are ordinarily very small; as noted earlier, banks have an incentive to invest excess reserves in interest-bearing assets and as they do so the money stock expands. But from about 1933 to 1945 excess reserves were substantial. Interest rates were very low during this period and so the incentive to invest excess reserves was small. Moreover, memories of the runs on banks in the early 1930s were fresh, leading banks to hold a cushion of excess reserves in the event of further runs. Thus, although the required reserve ratio is the major factor determining k, the experience of the 1930s makes clear that changes in excess reserves can be an important factor producing changes in k.

In addition to its value in studying money stock behavior historically, the analysis provides insight into the task faced by the central bank in controlling the money stock. If the central bank wants to stabilize the money stock, then it can change H through open-market operations as required to offset changes that may be occurring in h and/or in k. Thus, the Federal Reserve cannot be absolved from responsibility for the monetary contraction between 1929 and 1933; the Fed could have and should have increased the monetary base to offset increases in the currency ratio at that time.

This analysis also makes clear the potential costs in monetary instability resulting from reserve requirement regulations that make k unstable. In the simple examples discussed earlier it was assumed that the required reserve ratio was 0.2; in fact, however, there are different required reserve ratios for different size banks and for different types of deposits. Large banks have higher reserve requirements than small banks and demand deposits have higher requirements than time deposits. The reserve requirement regulations, therefore, make the *average* reserve requirement for the banking system as a whole change whenever funds are moved between large and small banks or between demand and time deposits. Since the reserve requirement regulations are the responsibility of the Federal Reserve, monetary instability resulting from instability in the average reserve requirement is also the Federal Reserve's responsibility.

While no distinction has been made in this discussion between the M_1 and M_2 definitions of the money stock, the analysis can be conducted using either definition. If the M_2 definition is used, D in the formula presented above is demand deposits plus time deposits, and k is the ratio of bank reserves to deposits so defined. If the M_1 definition is used, D is demand deposits and k is the ratio of bank reserves to demand deposits. Under current reserve requirement regulations, with either money definition k will fluctuate unless the ratio of demand to time deposits is constant, which it isn't.

SUMMARY

Since the money stock consists of currency plus bank deposits, changes in the quantity of money depend on the functioning of a number of separate elements in the monetary system. Since commercial banks hold reserves against deposits, deposits cannot change unless reserves change or the reserve ratio changes. Changes in the average reserve ratio arise from changes in reserve requirements, in excess reserves, and in the distribution of deposits in different size banks and between demand and time deposits.

Under the assumption of a constant reserve ratio, increases in bank reserves generate a multiple expansion of deposits, and decreases a multiple contraction. Total bank reserves can change through a flow of currency between the general public and the commercial banks or from open-market purchases or sales of government securities by the central bank which change the monetary base.

Treasury operations are best viewed *as if* all sales of securities are made to the general public. Although the central bank in fact buys government securities from the Treasury from time to time, it is convenient to suppose that the Treasury first sells the securities to the general public, and that the central bank then buys the securities from the general public. Viewed in this way, a government budget deficit financed by bonds, or a budget surplus used to retire bonds, does not affect bank reserves and the money stock. Central bank purchases (sales) of bonds, however, do increase (decrease) the monetary base. Thus the central bank, and not the Treasury, has the principal responsibility for all fluctuations that may occur in a nation's money stock.

SUGGESTION FOR FURTHER READING

Burger, Albert E., 1971. *The money supply process.* Belmont, Calif.: Wadsworth.

Monetary 7
Policy

In previous chapters a number of scientific issues have been analyzed, issues concerning how the world works. Monetary policy disputes frequently arise from differences of opinion on scientific issues which can, in principle, be resolved through advances in theory and the accumulation of additional evidence. But monetary policy disputes also depend on disputes over values. Even if it is agreed that policy A will produce effects X, and policy B effects Y, bitter disputes may arise over whether effects X are to be *preferred* to effects Y. Indeed, "preferred" is sometimes too mild a word; those advocating one policy may be accused by their opponents of being cruel, heartless, selfish, or worse.

Since policy arguments are frequently so heated, it is important to stand back as far as possible in an attempt to sort out the issues. Matters of preference must be separated from matters of science. *If* it is true that policy A will produce horrible effects Z instead of pleasant effects X, those who favor policy B producing merely unpleasant effects Y should not be accused of being insensitive and heartless. Unfortunately, however, the bearer of the bad news that policy A will not produce the pleasant effects X, and who therefore advocates policy B, all too often finds opponents attacking motives rather than providing counterevidence.

SCIENTIFIC ISSUES

The foundation for discussing the scientific part of policy issues has been established in the previous chapters. A review of that analysis will help to bring out the major policy issues.

In the long run an expansion of money growth will produce a higher rate of inflation. Interest rates will rise by the amount of the increase in inflation, and fluctuate around that higher level. The real rate of interest will not have changed. The level of unemployment, although affected during the transition to the long run, will not be permanently affected by the higher rate of money growth.

In the short run higher money growth or, rather, money growth higher than households and business firms expected and adjusted to, will tend to expand employment and output with relatively little initial effect on the price level. In the very short run the extra money growth may push interest rates down a little, but after a time this effect, if any, will be reversed as the rising level of business activity stimulates business and consumer credit demands.

During the transition from the short run to the long run, assuming that money growth stays at the new higher rate, business activity will slow. If money growth stimulates business activity in the short run but not in the long run, the transition from booming business activity to normal business activity must involve slower than normal business growth for a time.

As inflationary expectations develop, prices will rise. Indeed, because the price level rises by a lesser extent than required for long-run equilibrium during the initial period of higher money growth, the price level has some catching up to do to reflect the higher rate of money growth. The *rate* of price change—the inflation rate—will therefore be above the long-run rate during this phase of the adjustment. Interest rates will probably also be rising as inflationary expectations develop, although the extra credit demands during the boom may already have pushed interest rates close to their new long-run levels.

These points are summarized schematically in Fig. 7.1. In the bottom panel the money stock is assumed to be growing at a moderate rate during the initial equilibrium, and then suddenly to start growing at a higher rate which is maintained.

In the initial equilibrium the price level is growing gently, and the unemployment rate and the interest rate are both constant. When money growth rises, the price path is initially unaffected, as shown by the solid line rising at the same rate as before. (The dashed lines in the figure will be discussed later.) Initially, the interest rate falls a little.

As the monetary expansion "takes hold," the unemployment rate falls significantly and interest rates are bid up by rising credit demands. The price level begins to rise just a bit faster, but the acceleration may be so slight as to be hardly noticed. As the boom progresses, however, prices rise more rapidly and, with the development of inflationary expectations, so do interest rates.

As shown by the solid lines in Fig. 7.1, the boom eventually dies out and unemployment begins to rise back toward its long-run normal level. The price level continues to rise; indeed, in Fig. 7.1 the *rate* of inflation is shown to be rising for a time after the business cycle peak (the low point of the unemployment rate) and only after unemployment has increased substantially does the inflation rate begin to approach the new equilibrium inflation rate.

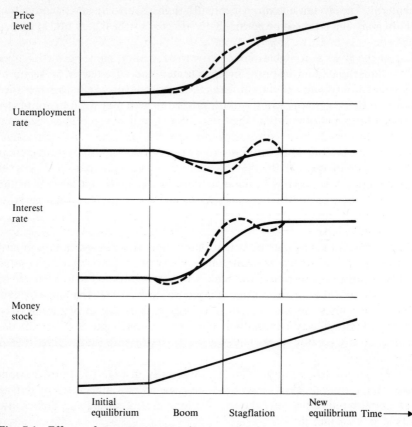

Fig. 7.1 Effects of monetary expansion.

The stagflation period is clearly an unhappy one. Unemployment is rising and so is the inflation rate. The interest rate, although falling as unemployment is rising, is much higher than it had been during the period of price stability. This combination of events seems difficult to understand because it seems inconsistent with the argument that weak markets *depress* prices. But consider this argument carefully. *If* the initial equilibrium and the new equilibrium have the characteristics shown, and *if* the boom is characterized by below-normal unemployment and by inflation below the new equilibrium rate, *then* the period between the boom and the new equilibrium *must* be characterized by rising unemployment and rising prices. There is no escape.

It should be emphasized that the solid lines present a schematic picture. In fact, prices, unemployment, interest, and money will be fluctuating around the solid lines, and the fluctuations are ordinarily large enough that the underlying patterns are difficult to see. Nevertheless, the basic patterns shown in Fig. 7.1 do emerge from a careful analysis of the data and are consistent with the predictions of economic theory.

The dashed lines in Fig. 7.1 depict a variation of the basic pattern. The same money growth path is assumed and the same long-run equilibrium. But the transition to the new long-run equilibrium may take a variety of forms. As compared with the solid lines, the dashed lines depict a more vigorous boom, (unemployment falls more) followed by a recession in which unemployment not only rises but rises to above-normal levels. With the more vigorous boom the rate of inflation rises more, and the characteristics of the stagflation period are even more unpleasant. The interest rate also fluctuates more because credit demands fluctuate with the level of economic activity.

A great variety of dashed paths could have been shown in the figure since the adjustment process of going from one long-run equilibrium to another takes a variety of forms.[1] But these patterns have in common (1) boom periods in which unemployment is on the average below normal; and (2) stagflation periods in which unemployment is on the average rising. In the early stages of the boom, at least, inflation is below its new equilibrium rate and in the latter stages of the boom and early stages of the stagflation inflation is above its new equilibrium rate.

This description of the effects of a sustained increase in the rate of growth of the money stock is not particularly controversial provided the qualifying phrase "other things equal" is not forgotten. But the analysis of the effects of monetary expansion *assuming* other things equal is not the same as the *assertion* that in analyzing historical business cycles other things were in fact equal or even approximately equal. Although evidence supporting the assertion was presented in previous chapters, the scientific side of policy disputes centers on claims that factors other than the stock of money have played, and will play, an important role in the business cycle process. Keeping in mind the possibility that the business cycle may reflect a mixture of monetary and nonmonetary disturbances, the basic issues surrounding short-run stabilization policy may now be examined.

SHORT-RUN STABILIZATION POLICY

If all other things were equal, as assumed in discussing Fig. 7.1, no one would consciously propose the acceleration of money growth shown in the figure because no one wants to impose the economic fluctuations character-

---

1 Put another way, economists do not know enough to be able to explain why the adjustment process takes particular forms, and so must fall back to the weak statement that many different patterns are possible.

izing the boom and stagflation periods in order eventually to reach a new equilibrium with the *same* rate of unemployment as before but a *higher* rate of inflation. But suppose a temporary monetary fluctuation is used to smooth out the undesirable effects of something else *not* being equal. This possibility is shown in Fig. 7.2.

The solid lines in Fig. 7.2 show the hypothesized effects of something else not being equal when money growth is held steady. Unemployment rises, interest rates rise, fall, and then rise again. The price level, which had been rising slowly, levels off, and then resumes its rise.

A successful monetary policy would respond to the disturbance by accelerating money growth as shown by the dashed line in the bottom panel of Fig. 7.2. Knowing that accelerated money growth lowers unemployment in the short run, other things equal, the employment effects of the disturbance can be partly or completely offset if money growth can be accelerated

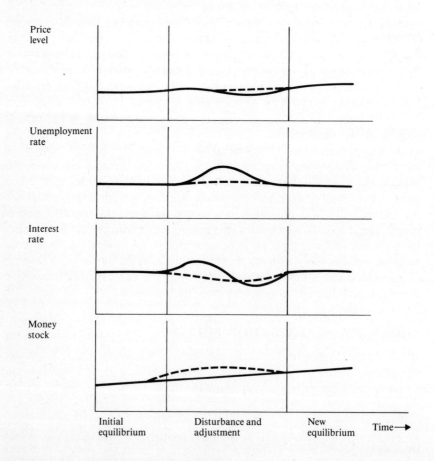

Fig. 7.2 Countercyclical monetary policy.

by the right amount at the right time. And then, as the disturbance disappears, or as the economy adjusts to the disturbance, money growth is slowed. The result is that the economic variables being analyzed follow the dashed paths; by making the money stock *less* stable, unemployment, prices, and interest are made more stable.

Now the nature of the policy problem can be seen clearly. Suppose the monetary authorities *think* there is a disturbance when there is not. Accelerating money growth as in the bottom panel of Fig. 7.2, instead of offsetting another disturbance, will itself be a disturbance and the economy will begin to follow the paths shown in Fig. 7.1. By the time the authorities recognize the mistake and slow money growth the damage will have been done because the forces set in motion generating the boom must be followed by the forces generating the stagflation. It *may* be possible to adjust policy to partly reverse the mistake and to reduce the unpleasantness of the stagflation stage, but since the precise nature of the short-run adjustment process is not well understood further policy action may worsen rather than improve the situation.

RELATIONSHIP OF MONETARY TO FISCAL POLICY

There are many dimensions to government tax and spending policies, but for the purposes at hand fiscal policy may be defined in terms of changes in the *amount* of government spending and in the *schedule* of tax rates. Because, by the government budget constraint, a government deficit must necessarily be financed by some combination of sales of government bonds and newly created base money, in sorting out fiscal from monetary policy effects it is important to analyze fiscal policy under the assumption that the level (or the path over time) of the monetary base is taken as given. Otherwise, the effects of fiscal policy—of changes in tax and spending policies—will be confounded with the effects of changes in monetary policy.

In the previous section it was argued that a countercyclical monetary policy would provide for faster monetary expansion when private demands would otherwise be weak and slower monetary expansion when private demands would otherwise be excessive. Exactly the same argument may be applied to fiscal policy: when the economy would otherwise be weak government spending may be increased to add directly to aggregate demand and/or tax rates reduced to stimulate private demand. The opposite policies may be followed when the economy would otherwise be excessively strong.

The argument for fiscal policy has tremendous surface appeal. If the construction industry is weak during a recession, what could be simpler and more effective than putting unemployed construction workers to work on government construction projects? But, if government spending on public works projects increases, where does the government obtain the funds and what are the effects of the government raising the funds?

Since fiscal policy is being analyzed, the government is assumed not to obtain the extra funds by expanding the money stock. What happens, then, when the government sells bonds to finance the new spending? A full treatment of this question is beyond the scope of this book but the basic issues involving the interaction of the effect of interest rate changes on the demand for money and on spending decisions can be outlined.

In Chapter 4, in the discussion on the effect of a change in the money stock on economic activity, it was argued that as a first approximation the amount of money people want to hold depends on the level of *nominal* income—and not separately on the levels of real income and prices. It was also argued that the cost of holding money has some effect, though a small one short of hyperinflation, on the amount of money people want to hold. Suppose for the moment that the interest rate has no effect on money demand. Then, the level of nominal income cannot change unless the money stock changes. When the government sells bonds to finance new public works expenditures, interest rates must rise sufficiently to choke off private interest-sensitive expenditures equal to the new government expenditures. The level of nominal income will be unchanged; government expenditures will simply displace private expenditures of the same amount.

We have argued, however, that the demand for money does depend on the interest rate to some extent, and so the extreme case just described cannot be strictly true. If the sale of government bonds raised interest rates a lot, perhaps people would want to hold much less money at any given level of nominal income; that is, the Cambridge k would be lower. For a given money stock (recall again our assumption that the money stock is held constant as we analyze fiscal policy) the level of nominal income could then be much higher. But will the sale of additional government bonds change interest rates very much?

The answer to this question depends on how sensitive private expenditures are to interest rates. Suppose private expenditures are highly sensitive to interest rates. Then, additional government spending will raise interest rates just a little because only a small increase will be sufficient to reduce private interest-sensitive expenditures by an amount almost equal to the increase in government expenditures. Total nominal income will rise a little, but not much. In the new equilibrium the slightly lower Cambridge k is consistent with the slightly higher interest rate.

The above analysis is unavoidably complex and no doubt confusing to many readers. But before rereading the preceding paragraphs, finish this one and the next also! The complexity stems from the interaction of two different interest elasticities—that of money demand and that of spending. If the interest elasticity of money demand is literally zero, then government spending cannot increase total nominal income at all; the only issue then is the *size* of the interest rate increase required to choke back, or crowd out, private expenditures equal to the new government spending. The increase in the interest rate will be large (small) if the interest elasticity of private expenditures is low (high).

If the interest elasticity of money demand is not literally zero (as it is not), then there is room for bond-financed government spending to expand total income. But suppose private spending is highly interest sensitive. Then, when the government sells bonds, only a tiny interest rate increase will choke back private expenditures in an almost equal amount.

There continues to be a lively argument in the economics profession over the sizes of money demand and spending interest elasticities. There is little question, however, that over the past quarter century the average of professional opinion has arrived at a reduced estimate of the money demand interest elasticity and an increased estimate of the spending interest elasticity, implying that fiscal policy is less effective than it was previously thought to be. At the present time economists who advocate active use of fiscal policy generally expect $1 of bond-financed government spending to increase total nominal GNP by $2 to $3, while monetarists generally expect an effect on total nominal GNP of $1 or less.

Whatever may be the correct estimate of the effect of government spending, political support for government spending is probably greater than would be the case if the preceding analysis were generally understood. Political support is generated by the highly visible effects of government spending itself (putting construction workers back to work on public works projects for example), but the indirect effects of crowding out private expenditures are highly dispersed, small for any one industry, and therefore hard to identify.

The discussion so far has concentrated on government spending, but with the analysis now in hand tax policy can be examined easily and quickly. Suppose the government cuts personal income taxes. If households respond by increasing their spending by the amount of the tax cut, then the previous analysis applies except that the extra spending is private rather than governmental. As before, the key question concerns the extent of the offset in interest-sensitive private spending.

If a tax cut does not induce extra spending by a household, then GNP will not rise. But do not fall into the trap of arguing that in this case the sale of government bonds will raise interest rates, choke back private interest-sensitive spending, and cause GNP actually to fall. If households are not spending a tax cut, they must be saving it. Households will be supplying these funds to the credit markets in amounts matching the government's demands for funds to finance the tax cut. Thus, interest rates won't increase and private interest-sensitive spending won't fall.

Whatever the size of the effect of government spending on nominal income, it is important to understand that an increase in bond-financed government spending (or tax cuts) can only raise the *level* of nominal GNP and not its *rate of growth*. Only if the "dosage" were continuously increased could fiscal policy generate continuous growth in nominal income, but continuously rising deficits (rising more rapidly than the trend rate of increase in nominal GNP) are certain to cause trouble eventually. If the amount of government bonds outstanding gets large enough, there will eventually be fears that the government will not be able to continue to pay the interest on the government debt. At that stage the government will not be able to sell additional bonds, and may have trouble refinancing maturing issues of old bonds. When a situation of this type occurs at a time when the government is weak for other reasons, money creation is likely to be the only resort if the government is to pay its bills and redeem its maturing debt. The result is hyperinflation.

It is in a situation of this type that inflation may be said to cause money growth. If the government is unwilling or unable to reduce the number of its employees and the volume of materials and supplies it purchases, then wage and price increases will generate increases in government spending. For example, if the government is to maintain police and fire protection, it must be willing to raise wages at about the same rate at which wages are rising in the private economy to prevent employees in the police and fire departments from quitting to take higher paying jobs elsewhere.

In hyperinflation it is generally true that increases in tax revenues do not match increases in the price level because taxpayers, naturally enough, delay tax payments in order to reduce the real value of the taxes paid.[2] Since the government cannot sell bonds in this environment, in desperation it turns to money creation to finance essential public services. Extra inflation, therefore, causes extra money growth which in turn generates further inflation until the monetary system breaks down completely.

In these circumstances, then, it might be said that in any particular month inflation causes money growth but that, more fundamentally, it is a monetary system in which the government has lost control of money creation that causes the inflation. Since modern governments so frequently resort to deficit finance, it is extremely important that public confidence in the credit-worthiness of the government be maintained so that deficits can be financed through bonds rather than through money creation.

The United States is far from this dangerous situation, although warning flags are now being hoisted because of the immense size of the United States Government's future Social Security obligations. The purpose of these comments, however, is not to raise warning flags; rather, the purpose is to show that government budget deficits beyond a certain point must be regarded as an essentially temporary phenomenon. Tax rates must be set at levels that on average will yield enough revenues to cover government

---

2   Penalties for late payment of taxes are typically set by law in nominal terms. The real value of these penalties is rapidly eroded by hyperinflation, and courts rarely restate the penalties to reflect inflation.

spending. Large budget deficits cannot be used as a permanent policy because eventually the credit-worthiness of the government itself will become questionable. Thus not only must fiscal policy be evaluated in terms of the extent of the crowding out of private expenditures but also in terms of whether the particular fiscal measures being considered strengthen or weaken the prospect that the private economy will itself maintain full employment once the fiscal stimulus is removed. These longer run issues are extremely important but tend to be lost in the heat of current political debate. It is simply not true, however, that these bridges can be crossed when they are reached in the future, as New York City has discovered in recent years.

This analysis of fiscal policy has touched only the surface of a large and controversial subject. There are significant disagreements concerning the analysis of temporary versus permanent tax changes, sales versus income tax changes, various types of business taxes, the general design of the tax system, the efficiency of countercyclical government spending, the prospects for improved timing of fiscal policy changes, and many other important issues. Only the three basic issues that relate most directly to monetarism have been discussed here. Those issues are: (1) the importance of analyzing fiscal policy under the assumption of bond financing of budget deficits in order not to confuse fiscal and monetary effects; (2) the fact that the net effect of fiscal policy on nominal GNP depends on the extent to which private spending changes induced by government bond sales offset the effects of fiscal policy changes; and (3) the necessarily temporary (nonpermanent) nature of large government budget deficits, which requires, ultimately, acceptance of the level of GNP produced without reliance on fiscal stimulus.

HISTORICAL EVALUATION OF MONETARY POLICY

In principle it is clear that monetary policy adjustments may or may not be stabilizing, depending on the nature of market responses to policy adjustments and on the skill of the policymakers. In forming an opinion on the advisability of an activist monetary policy which makes frequent adjustments in money growth in an effort to offset disturbances in various sectors of the economy, a key input is an historical evaluation of policy successes and failures.

The historical evaluation of monetary policy has an easy part and a hard part. It is relatively easy to describe, or characterize, policy but relatively difficult to show that particular policy adjustments made the situation better or worse than it otherwise would have been. Let us begin with the easy part.

In this book monetary policy has been discussed under the assumption that the central bank controls the money stock, or could control it if desired. While a reasonably complete technical discussion of money control issues goes beyond the confines of this book, the general nature of the problem was discussed in Chapter 6.

While central banks frequently have not controlled the money stock, the technical means to regulate the quantity of money exist, and always have existed. Thus, even though the money stock may have been out of control in a particular situation because, for example, the government was too weak to take decisive action, the fact that money was not controlled speaks to the politics of the situation and not to the economics of money stock control. Therefore, our assumption that the central bank controls the money stock covers both deliberate control and lack of deliberate control due to the pursuit of other objectives. If the central bank does not in fact push the button, it should nevertheless be held responsible for permitting someone else to push the button.

This point is important enough to warrant further discussion. Monetary instability is sometimes excused on the ground that the money stock could not be controlled because of the costs of doing so. This argument is valid insofar as it represents a plea to examine both the costs and the benefits of reducing monetary instability. But such an examination, which may show a balance of either net benefits or net costs, is the opposite of the refusal to analyze costs and benefits implied by the assertion that the money stock could not be controlled in a particular set of circumstances.

Once it is agreed that the central bank or, more generally, the central government ought to be held responsible for monetary instability, then a large number of cases can be cited in which the instability was clearly and unambiguously harmful. Easy and obvious examples are the hyperinflations discussed in Chapter 2. An example from United States history is the monetary contraction from 1929 to 1933 which shows up clearly in Fig. 2.1. It is possible, though not in my opinion correct, to argue that the 1929–1933 monetary contraction had little to do with causing the Great Depression, but it can make no sense whatsoever to argue that the monetary contraction was helpful. The monetary contraction clearly and unambiguously worked in the wrong direction and provided no offsetting benefits. At the time, however, it was thought that the monetary policy being followed would help to retain the gold standard, but the United States went off the gold standard domestically in 1933 anyway.

In Chapter 4 it was argued that the pronounced and regular procyclical pattern of the money stock (shown in Fig. 4.1) has had much to do with causing business cycle fluctuations. Even if this statement is disputed, it is hard to imagine that this monetary behavior has been helpful; that is, even if it is argued that the business cycle is basically caused by nonmonetary factors, monetary policy has systematically amplified rather than damped the cycle. In assessing monetary policy, disputes do not revolve around the *fact* of the procyclical behavior of the money stock but rather around the reasons for this behavior and claims that offsetting benefits are realized, particularly the claimed benefit of greater interest rate stability. This claim is so important to disputes about monetary policy that it deserves a separate section.

THE ROLE OF INTEREST RATES IN MONETARY POLICY

The procyclical behavior of the money stock in the United States reflects the unfortunate fact that the Federal Reserve System has never paid much attention to controlling money. The Fed has, instead, viewed its job as that of controlling, or influencing, interest rates. Before discussing the reasons for this policy, its role in generating the procyclical pattern to the money stock will be described.

To begin the story, consider the Federal Reserve's policy problem during the early stage of a business cycle expansion. Unemployment, though falling, is relatively high as a result of the previous recession. Because unemployment is high, the Fed is very concerned about maintaining the pace of business expansion. Also, because of the previous recession and the relatively high rate of unemployment, the rate of inflation is gradually drifting down and there appears to be no reason to follow a restrictive monetary policy to "fight inflation."

As the business recovery proceeds, rising credit demands generate upward pressures on interest rates. The Fed, underestimating the role of credit *demands* in pushing up interest rates, interprets the rate increases as reflecting a contraction of credit *supplies* which, if not offset, will choke back spending on housing, consumer durables, plants and equipment, and other expenditures customarily financed by borrowed funds. Thus, the Fed responds to rising interest rates by expanding *its* supply of funds by purchasing government bonds. When the Fed buys government bonds, bank reserves and the money stock rise.

But since the upward pressure on interest rates is caused by expanding credit demands in an expanding economy, the rising money growth adds to the economy's upward momentum. As the business expansion proceeds, the Fed decides that a little monetary restraint is in order, and so it raises its interest rate target. But when a policy of restraint is first adopted only mild restraint seems needed, and so the interest rate targets are raised only a little. Moreover, if rising credit demands are tending to push rates up faster than the Fed's interest rate targets are rising, as so often happens, then the Fed will continue to add to the supply of funds, and therefore to the money stock, as it cushions what it believes to be excessively rapid increases in interest rates. At this stage of the business cycle the Fed is continuing to feed money into an expanding economy.

As the expansion proceeds, and perhaps turns into an inflationary boom, the Fed becomes increasingly concerned about inflation and less and less concerned about unemployment. Interest rate targets are raised, and raised again. Eventually the Fed's interest rate targets rise more rapidly than credit demands and money growth begins to slow. But the effect of slower money growth on economic activity appears with a lag. The economy continues to boom and the Fed's concern over inflation continues to rise. Interest rate targets are increased further, and money growth slows even more.

Eventually the slower money growth takes hold and the economy begins to decline. As the economy begins to decline, credit demands slacken and interest rates tend to fall. However, the economy still appears very strong. Unemployment is low, even if it is beginning to rise. Because the statistics arrive with a lag, and because the statistics have an overlay of random fluctuation, the weakness in the economy is not immediately recognized. To maintain the high interest rates "to fight inflation" when credit demands are falling, additional monetary contraction is required, adding to the contractionary pressures already operating.

Reviewing the argument so far, money growth is relatively high during the expansion phase of the cycle as the Fed cushions upward pressures on interest rates. Eventually, however, the Fed becomes sufficiently concerned about inflation that its interest rate targets are raised enough to slow money growth. The slower money growth, after a time, produces a business slowdown. As credit demands weaken, money growth is further contracted to keep interest rates from falling "too fast." The additional slowdown in money growth turns the business slowdown into a business downturn, and another recession is underway.

As the recession proceeds, interest rates tend to fall rapidly. If the Fed cushions the fall, then money growth will continue to decline, adding to the recessionary momentum. Now the story runs in reverse. Eventually the Fed becomes concerned enough about the recession to push its interest rate targets down enough to outpace the falling credit demands. Money growth stabilizes, and then turns up. With the end of the contractionary monetary policy, business activity turns up. We are now back to the beginning of the story, ready for another cyclical expansion fueled by rising money growth and later to be stopped by falling money growth.

The procyclical pattern to the money stock has been observed so often and is so well documented that it is astonishing that the Federal Reserve permits the pattern to continue. Yet, in mid-1977 the typical pattern was appearing again. Money growth was higher in the second four quarters of recovery—1976:I-1977:I—than it was in the first four quarters—1975:I-1976:I—and money growth appears to have accelerated further after the first quarter of 1977. Why does the Federal Reserve cause, or permit, this procyclical pattern to appear again and again?

REASONS FOR MONETARY INSTABILITY

The proximate answer to the question just posed is the Federal Reserve's attachment to interest rate targets, but the reasons for this attachment have varied from time to time. The four most important of these reasons will now be discussed one by one, followed by an overall evaluation of the issues involved.

Financing War

During World Wars I and II monetary policy was subordinated to the needs of the Treasury in financing the large government budget deficits caused by a more rapid expansion in wartime expenditures than in wartime taxes. When sales of new government bonds threatened to increase interest rates unduly, the Fed would purchase some of the bonds. Indeed, in World War II this policy was pushed to the point that the Fed was committed to peg the long-term bond rate at 2.5 percent. The Fed purchased any and all government bonds offered at that rate, and a rapid increase in the money stock after 1941 was the result. (See Fig. 2.2.) During the Korean and Vietnam Wars the Federal Reserve also permitted rapid monetary expansion in the process of attempting to help the Treasury finance deficits.

Interest Rate Smoothing

Since the Korean War an important aspect of Federal Reserve policy has been its attempt to smooth, or cushion, short-run fluctuations in interest rates. Both credit demands and credit supplies are subject to short-run random fluctuations for a great variety of reasons. Interest rates, and prices in individual markets generally, bounce around a lot. Unpredictable price fluctuations disrupt planning, and so it seems perfectly natural to argue that a price increase followed shortly by a price decrease serves no useful purpose. Doesn't the Federal Reserve perform a valuable service when it smooths out unnecessary and "disorderly" short-run fluctuations in interest rates?

There are two aspects to this argument. First, it is simply not true that short-run price and interest rate fluctuations serve no useful purpose. Underlying the fluctuations are supply-and-demand changes that must somehow be equilibrated. A detailed analysis of the changes themselves is required before government action to stabilize the market can be justified. If government intervention to stabilize a market involves a subsidy to the buyers and/or sellers (and intervention almost always does involve a subsidy, at least to the extent of the government administrative costs involved), then justification of the intervention requires justification of a *general* taxpayer subsidy to the participants in a *particular* market.

The second aspect to this argument is that whatever the benefits of price smoothing it must be shown that government intervention of the type considered will in fact produce the desired smoothing. There is a strong case to be made that Federal Reserve attempts to stabilize interest rates have actually served to destabilize them. On a day-by-day, week-by-week basis it is extremely difficult to distinguish an interest rate change that will be reversed in the near future from one reflecting longer run changes in credit demands. The evidence is quite clear that on the average the Federal Reserve has failed to distinguish temporary from longer run pressures on interest rates. The result is a procyclical pattern to the money stock. This behavior of the money stock has made the economy less stable and, therefore, has made credit demands and interest rates less stable. The Federal Reserve *may* have made day-to-day interest rate changes smaller but it has made peak-to-trough and trough-to-peak changes in interest rates over the course of the business cycle larger. For most participants in the bond and money markets the Fed has at best diminished the importance of a minor nuisance and has substituted instead a major problem.

Reducing Balance-of-Payments Deficits

In the early 1960s the Fed attempted to keep interest rates from falling in order to reduce the amount of capital flowing abroad to be invested at interest rates above United States rates. At that time the United States had a substantial international balance-of-payments deficit and was committed to maintain the international gold exchange standard that had been established in 1945. The flow of private capital abroad led to an outflow of monetary gold. The Kennedy Administration and the Federal Reserve were both concerned that the United States gold stock would be exhausted, which would make it impossible to continue to meet the commitment to sell gold at $35 per ounce. A similar consideration was responsible for the Fed's efforts to hold interest rates up in the early 1930s, but in the early 1960s, fortunately, a substantial monetary contraction did not result.

Stabilizing Thrift Institutions and Housing Construction

Another consideration that has been important ever since the 1966 "credit crunch" is the concern that rising market interest rates will lead savings and loan and mutual savings bank depositors to withdraw funds, reducing the funds available for home mortgage lending, and weakening—possibly bankrupting—certain savings and loan associations and mutual savings banks. The political strength of the thrift institutions and of the housing lobbies has also played a role in this matter.

Evaluating the Arguments

This catalog of reasons for Federal Reserve efforts to cushion interest rate movements could be substantially extended, but it is unnecessary to do so for present purposes. Examination of these and other cases suggests a more general explanation. Individual households and firms are directly affected by interest rate changes: economic behavior depends directly on prices. Economywide aggregates of quantities per se are of no significance to individuals. For example, to a motorist who drives up to the gas pump the price of gasoline matters but the motorist could not care less about total annual gasoline sales. Similarly, the homebuyer is affected by the mortgage rate but not by the total dollar amount of mortgage lending. To the individual, the connection between the total money stock and the general price level and interest rates is abstract and abstruse.

The political pressures falling on government policymakers reflect the failure of the electorate to understand the role of the money stock in generating observed price and interest rate movements. Moreover, policymakers themselves are not immune to the popular misconceptions. But rather than assuming that monetary instability reflects blind mistakes, it is worth toting up the benefits as well as the costs.

The most difficult situation to assess is that of wartime monetary expansion. During a major war a significant share of national output is diverted to war production. The incomes paid in the form of wages obviously cannot all be spent on consumption goods. The goods simply are not being produced. One way of preventing people from attempting to buy more goods than are available is to levy high taxes; a second is to permit interest rates to go high enough that people are willing to defer consumption and buy government bonds under the expectation that the bonds can be sold after the war and consumption then increased.

A third possibility is to rely on direct production controls to limit the availability of consumption goods, and on price controls with rationing to distribute the available consumption goods. Monetary expansion can then be used to finance the government budget deficit, and because consumption goods are unavailable people will simply accumulate money balances expecting to be able to buy goods after the war.

During World War II the United States relied on the first and third methods. Taxes were raised but not by enough to cover all wartime expenditures. Interest rates were pegged and whatever part of the budget deficit could not be met by borrowing at the pegged rates was met by monetary expansion.

People who accumulated money and/or bonds thought they would be able to exchange these to obtain goods after the war. But they were mistaken. The purchasing power represented by these bonds and money balances, at the goods prices prevailing during the war, could *never* be turned into goods, for the goods represented were irretrievably lost in the war effort. This loss would have been honestly reflected by wartime tax increases sufficient to pay for the war; then apparent purchasing power in the form of government bonds and money balances would not have been accumulated.

Would high taxes have stifled the war production effort? Would people have worked long hours of overtime if high income taxes had taken most of the earnings from the extra effort? The answers are unclear. But it is at least arguable that it was better to fool people into greater effort by paying them, in effect, in government bonds and cash balances that could not be spent and which never would buy the goods that people thought they would. The shock of the postwar inflation that eroded the purchasing power of accumulated savings could wait. The important thing was to get the production and win the war.

There are two problems with this argument. First, the wartime policy was manifestly discriminatory. Those who understood the implications of wartime finance protected themselves by buying land and anything else that was likely to retain its real value during an inflation; government bonds and money balances were avoided. Thus, the bonds and money balances were accumulated by the less educated and by those particularly susceptible to patriotic appeals and pressures to buy government bonds.

Second, a policy that depends on people being fooled is dangerous in a democratic society. If people catch on, the policy will fail. If people had realized in 1942 what would happen to the purchasing power of government bonds, the government could not have sold the bonds and would have had to finance the entire deficit through money creation. The resulting hyperinflation would have disrupted the production process and reduced the moral authority of the government, making it more difficult to persuade the public to bear the sacrifices of war.

All things considered, is inflationary finance a good policy under the extreme pressures of a major war? The answer just is not clear.

But for small wars the answer is much easier. Monetary expansion during the Vietnam War clearly added economic problems to an already difficult situation. By the time American involvement began to decline, the United States economy was suffering from an entrenched rate of inflation of five to six percent and inflationary expectations were well developed. Interest rates, far from being cushioned by monetary expansion, had risen to levels considerably higher than those prevailing in 1965.

What were the benefits? The acceleration of money growth in the second half of 1965 delayed interest rate increases by a few months. The sharp reduction in money growth in 1966, though overdone, did slow the economy and check inflation. But these gains were tossed away by continued high money growth in 1967–1968. The thrift institutions and the housing industry were not in the end protected; by permitting money growth to run high and inflation to develop, interest rates were bid to higher levels than they would have attained with steady, moderate money growth. Severe "crunches" hit these industries in 1966 and 1969. The monetary policy of smoothing interest rates day by day, by losing control over the money stock, amplified the magnitude of interest rate swings over longer periods.

To summarize this discussion, for reasons that vary greatly from one time to another, the Federal Reserve has always resisted interest rate movements until the pressures and the observed rate of money growth become too large to ignore. This process has not permitted money growth to get completely out of control, except for the disastrous monetary contraction from 1929 to 1933. But the resulting monetary instability has been costly. In exchange for the temporary benefit of avoiding sharp interest rate changes for a few months, monetary instability has generated substantial inflations and significant business cycle fluctuations.

FEDERAL RESERVE PREFERENCES

It is sometimes argued that Federal Reserve policy cannot be properly understood without paying attention to the "central banker bias" against inflation and "central banker insensitivity" to unemployment. This view may have had some validity before World War II, but not in the period since.

First, if the Federal Reserve has had different preferences than those of the political party in power, the differences cannot have been very marked. An examination of Federal Reserve policy actions does not suggest that either monetary policy actions or intentions have systematically become restrictive before fiscal policy actions, or have remained restrictive longer.

Second, even though members of the Board of Governors of the Federal Reserve System have 14-year terms, resignations have been frequent enough that a President has always had the opportunity to create a more expansionist, or contractionist, board if he wanted to do so.

Third, over the years numerous bills have been offered in Congress to tighten congressional and administration control over the Fed but, with the exception of House Concurrent Resolution 133 (discussed below), no legislation of any significance has even come close to passage. It just does not make sense to argue that the Fed has been able to go its own way in opposition to the President and Congress given the lack of interest Presidents and Congresses have shown in changing matters.

Finally, it should be emphasized that the Federal Reserve consults frequently and regularly with the President and his top officials and advisers. Differences of opinion have, naturally, existed but they are probably not atypical of intragovernmental differences generally. The Fed does have more independence on paper than other agencies, but this fact should not be overemphasized. In fact, given the political power of the organized interests connected with other agencies, a President may have more actual power over monetary policy than he has over policy in many other areas.

MONETARY POLICY RULES VERSUS DISCRETION

From the long experience with monetary instability some economists have come to the conclusion that the central bank should be constrained by a legislated rule requiring that a specified rate of growth of money be maintained. This is the position favoring *rules*.

Other economists argue against policy rules. Some fear that providing for legislative determination of money growth will politicize monetary policy and lead to even more instability. Others argue that policy has not been nearly as bad as claimed in the previous sections, and that rather than give up on an active, discretionary policy, we should work to improve policy. Whenever steady money growth is the best policy, discretionary policymakers can voluntarily adopt that policy without losing flexibility as a result of legislated policy rules. This is the position favoring *discretion*.

There are three basic arguments for legislated monetary rules. One is political: that in a democratic society public officials should be regulated by laws debated and enacted by the elected legislature. Officials ought not to be given broad grants of power and merely instructed to act in the "public interest." The possibility of capricious and arbitrary actions by public officials is too great; hidden pressures from special interest groups and abuse of power are too common to be ignored. Why should monetary officials be any different in these respects from other government officials? Indeed, all government officials should be more tightly constrained by precise legislated rules than is the norm today.

A second argument for monetary rules is that discretionary policy-makers have made too many mistakes, and too many of the *same* mistakes, over the years for claims of the perfectibility of policy to be credible. At present, however, the argument is incomplete. While there is ample evidence of policy failures, there is no theory of why policymakers behave as they do.

The importance of this point can be seen through an analogy. The economic theory of the firm provides an explanation of why firms behave as they do. With the explanation afforded by theory, we can have a considerable degree of confidence that observed empirical regularities of private market behavior will continue into the future. But we have no satisfactory theory of the behavior of government agencies. Thus it may indeed be possible to perfect (or improve) the performance of the Federal Reserve even though the record is not encouraging.

The third reason for favoring monetary policy rules is subtle and difficult to understand: for discretionary policy adjustments to be effective, the policymakers must be able to predict the responses of households and firms to policy adjustments. But households and firms, in making *their* plans, must form predictions as to what the policymakers are going to do. Each side may, so to speak, end up playing a game: side 1 is guessing what side 2 is guessing side 1 will do, and so forth, and vice versa!

The implication of this argument is that a policy cannot possibly be optimal unless households and firms are in fact *correctly* predicting what the monetary authorities are doing. If not, households and firms will change their economic behavior as they learn what the monetary authorities are doing, and the same policy cannot, in general, be optimal when households and firms have changed their behavior.

This argument supports the proponents of rules because the only way to ensure that households and firms are responding to correct predictions of the actions of the monetary authorities is to announce the policy actions in advance and for the authorities to abide by the announcements. The best way to ensure that officials act in this way is to require by law that they do so.

Until 1975 Congress never made an attempt to oversee Federal Reserve policy. In the Federal Reserve Act the Fed is, in effect, simply instructed to serve the public interest. Not until House Concurrent Resolution 133, passed in February 1975, did the Congress even ask to be *informed* about Federal Reserve policy plans, much less control those plans through legislation.

The weak nature of Congressional interest in monetary policy is nicely illustrated by H.C.R. 133. The resolution provides for quarterly hearings alternating between the House and Senate Banking Committees in which the Federal Reserve reports money growth targets for the next 12 months. The resolution is completely silent on technical details, such as the statistical definition of money to be used. It provides no policy prescription as to the target rate of growth of money and says nothing about the Federal Reserve having an obligation to achieve the announced targets.

The Federal Reserve responded initially by announcing targets for *four* different monetary totals—M_1, M_2, M_3, and the so-called credit proxy, which it quietly dropped at a later quarterly hearing. There are substantial technical problems with the way the targets are defined, and the Fed has not always reached its announced targets.

At this time it is difficult to know whether H.C.R. 133 will be of any lasting significance. On the one hand, even though the resolution is silent on the extent of the Fed's obligation to hit its announced targets, it seems reasonable to believe that the Fed must feel at least somewhat constrained to hit the targets. If so, the worst extremes of monetary instability should be reduced because announced targets will always be "sensible" and "reasonable," which in political and bureaucratic practice means not changing very much. On the other hand, with several monetary targets each expressed as a range, 4.5–6.5 percent M_1 growth, for example, the quarterly hearings may turn out to be little more than a bewildering (to the Congress and general public) and meaningless bureaucratic exercise.

The rules versus discretion dispute is sometimes debated on misleadingly extreme definitions of "rules." A rule should not be interpreted as providing for every detail of monetary management for all time. Legislated rules can and ought to be changed from time to time as conditions change and knowledge accumulates. The most important part of the argument for rules is that pertaining to a known legislated provision for a specific rate of money growth; the damage is done by permitting the monetary authorities to muddle along, making day-by-day decisions that generate an unpredictable rate of money growth.

A legislated rule might be changed annually, or even more often, though the available evidence strongly suggests that stability of money growth over much longer periods of time would be desirable. Any legislated rule would have to leave some discretion with the central bank if only because monetary control to the dollar is impossible due to data inaccuracies and revisions.

SUMMARY

The general nature of the effects of changes in money growth, *other things equal*, is not a major source of dispute. However, attempts to use this knowledge to offset disturbances elsewhere in the economy is at the heart of debates over policy. For policy adjustments to be effective, policymakers must be able to identify disturbances in the private economy in time for their effects to be offset by deliberate changes in money growth.

Fiscal policy—that is, changes in government spending and tax rates—should be analyzed under the assumption of a given monetary policy. Changes in fiscal policy affect the size of the government budget deficit and, therefore, the amount of new bonds being sold to finance the deficit. An increase in bond-financed government spending directly stimulates economic activity, but this direct effect is partially and perhaps even largely offset by the depressing effects on private expenditures of the interest rate increases caused by the sale of government bonds. Financing new government spending by money creation avoids this offset in the short run, but the stimulating effect of such a policy is mostly the result of the money creation. In the long run such a policy will, of course, affect the price level rather than the level of real GNP.

An historical evaluation of monetary policy in the United States strongly suggests that monetary changes have more often themselves been disturbances rather than offsets to other disturbances. The *regularity* of the procyclical behavior of monetary fluctuations is particularly disturbing. This regularity is almost certainly due to an excessive emphasis on interest rates.

Efforts to smooth interest rate fluctuations have been motivated by a variety of factors ranging from minimizing the Treasury's interest expense in floating bonds to finance wartime expenditures to attempting to avoid the adverse effects of interest rate increases on home-building. In addition, the Federal Reserve has a standing policy of attempting to cushion all interest rate changes by monetary expansion or contraction.

The policy of cushioning interest rate changes is predicated on the view that interest rate fluctuations per se are harmful, and that most such fluctuations are, in the short run, the result of disturbances in the credit markets that ought to be offset by monetary fluctuations. However, this policy feeds *demand*-induced changes in the credit markets, leading to the typical procyclical pattern of money growth that aggravates business cycle fluctuations.

As a result of this experience, some economists have called for a legislated monetary rule to reduce monetary instability. Other economists favor continued reliance on discretion by the monetary authorities.

SUGGESTIONS FOR FURTHER READING

Friedman, Milton, 1959. *A program for monetary stability*. New York: Fordham University Press.

———, 1968. The role of monetary policy, *American Economic Review* **58** (March): 1–17.

Johnson, Harry G., 1964. Should there be an independent monetary authority? *The Federal Reserve System after Fifty Years*. (Hearings before the Subcommittee on Domestic Finance, Committee on Banking and Currency, House of Representatives, 88th Congress, 2nd session.) Washington: United States Government Printing Office, pp. 970–973.

Index

Aggregate demand, 60-61
Anticipatory effects, 30, 32-33, 39, 40, 47

Balance sheets
   commercial banks, 78-81
   Federal Reserve Banks, 86-87
Balance-of-payments deficits, 108
Bank deposits; *see* Deposits
Bank failures, 85n, 91
Bank notes, 85n
Bank reserves
   borrowed, 88
   as central bank liabilities, 85
   excess, 82-83, 88, 91
   required, 82, 90n, 91-92
Base money; *see* Monetary base
Bills
   defined, 68
   interest rates on; *see* Interest rates
Bonds
   coupon rate, 68
   defined, 68
   interest rates on; *see* Interest rates
Borrowing, by banks, 83, 88
Budget constraint, 34, 37, 99
Burger, Albert E., 93n
Business cycle
   defined, 42
   expansions and contractions, 42-44
   and interest rates, 73, 74-76, 95-97, 105
   and money growth, 42-44, 75, 95-97, 105-106

Cagan, Phillip, 11n, 22n
Cambridge k, 17, 20-21, 25, 40, 49, 51, 61, 100
Cash; *see* Currency; Money
Causation, direction of, 32, 45-47, 102
Central bank, 37, 45, 47, 84-88
   see also Federal Reserve System
Check clearing process, 82-83, 85
Checking accounts; *see* Deposits, demand
Commercial banks
   balance sheets, 78-81
   deposit expansion analysis, 82-84
   failures, 85n, 91
   reserves; *see* Bank reserves
Compound interest, 67
Consumer Price Index in United States, 30, 31, 58
Credit crunches, 108, 110
Credit proxy, 113
Crowding out effect, 100, 103
Currency
   bank notes, 85n
   as central bank liability, 84-85
   Federal Reserve notes, 84, 86-87, 90
   as ratio to money, 90
   reform, 25-26
   see also Money
Currency reform money, 25

Dean, Edwin, 23n
Deficit financing, 34, 89, 102-103, 107

Deficit money, 33-36
Demand deposits; *see* Deposits, de-
  mand
Demand for money, 12-16, 24-25, 47-
  50, 59-60, 90, 100-101
Deposits
  demand, 49, 77, 92
  expansion of, 82-84, 90-91
  time and savings, 49, 92
  Treasury, 88-90
Depressions; *see* Recessions
Discount loan, 68
Discount rate, 66
Distribution effects, 27-28
Dollar denominated assets, 27

Economic policy; *see* Fiscal policy;
  Monetary policy
Employment; *see* Unemployment
Equation of exchange, 17-20

Fama, Eugene F., 72n, 76n
Federal funds, 83
Federal Reserve Notes, 84, 86-87, 90
Federal Reserve System
  balance sheets, 86-87
  discount rate, 66
  Historical Chart book, 51
  independence, 111
  open market operations, 37, 88
  policy, 94-115
  reserve requirements, 82, 90n, 91-
    92
Fiscal policy, 99-103
Fiscalists, 1
Fisher, Irving, 17
Friedman, Milton, 64n, 115n

GNP; *see* Gross National Product
German inflation, 5, 11, 12, 33
Gold, 46, 84, 85, 104, 108
Government
  bonds, 27, 34-35, 49
  budget constraint, 34, 37, 99
  deficit financing, 34, 89, 102-103,
    107
  spending and inflation, 36
  see also Fiscal policy
Graham, Frank D., 23n
Great Depression, 104

Gross national product
  in current dollars, 51, 101, 103
  real, 10, 19-20, 44

Helicopter money, 26-33, 35
High-powered money, 90
  see also Monetary base
Historical Statistics of the United
  States, 22n
House Concurrent Resolution, 111,
  113, 133
Hungarian inflation, 11, 13
Hyperinflation, 5-6, 11-17, 45, 63,
  102, 110

Income, 48, 50
  see also Gross national product
Inflation
  causes of, 6, 38
  equilibrium, 38-40, 55-56
  in Germany, 5, 11, 12, 33
  in Hungary, 11, 13
  hyper-, 5-6, 11-17, 45, 63, 102,
    110
  importance of price of imported oil
    in, 30, 57, 61-62
  and interest rates, 70-74
  in Poland, 15
  redistribution effects of, 28
  in Russia, 14
  self-generating, 40
  in United States, 7-11, 29-31, 57-
    59, 61-62, 72-74
  wealth effects of, 28, 74
Institutions, monetary determinants
  of, 2
Interest rates
  arithmetic of, 65-67
  on bills, 68
  on bonds, 68
  business activity and, 73, 74-76,
    95-97, 105
  effect of on money demand, 61
  on federal funds, 66, 83
  inflation and, 70-74
  levels of in United States, 66, 73
  monetary policy and, 105-106
  on mortgages, 68
  real versus nominal 69-74
  on savings accounts, 67-68

Johnson, Harry G., 115n

Keynes, John Maynard, 46
Keynesianism, 1-2

Lucas, Robert E., Jr., 64n
Luxury goods prices, 28-29

Marshall, Alfred, 17
Mayer, Thomas, 4n
Monetarism, 1-3
Monetary base, 90-92
Monetary policy, 94-115
    historical evaluation of, 103=104
    and interest rates, 105-106
    rules versus discretion, 111-113
    scientific versus normative issues, 3,
        94
Money
    behavior of over business cycle, 42-
        44, 75, 95-97, 105-106
    control of, 3, 91, 103-104
    definitions of, 26, 43, 51-52, 92
    demand for, 12-16, 24-25, 47-50
        59-60, 90, 100-101
    and inflation, 11-17, 29-30, 36, 75,
        95-97
    instability of, 62, 91, 104, 106-110
    and interest rates, 75, 95-97
    quantity theory of, 17-21
    real quantity of, 17, 32, 36
    scarcity of, 6, 16-17
    target growth ranges of, 113
    velocity of, 18-21, 49, 51-52
Money stock
    in Germany, 12, 24, 33
    in Hungary, 13
    in Poland, 15
    in Russia, 14
    in United States, 7, 10, 29-31, 41,
        43-44, 51
Mortgages, 49

National output; see Income, Gross
    national product
Natural experiments, 45-46
Necessities goods pieces, 29

OPEC, 30, 57, 61-62
Open market money, 37-38

Open market operations, 37, 88
Output; see Income, Gross national
    product

Polish inflation, 15
Poole, William, 43n, 64n
Price adjustment process, 28-31, 36,
    52-54, 95-97
Price index
    in Germany, 12, 33
    in Hungary, 13
    in Poland, 15
    in Russia, 14
    in United States, 7, 30, 31, 58

Quantity theory of money, 17-22

Recessions, 43, 55, 57, 61, 106
Recoveries, 43, 106
Reserve requirements, 82, 90n, 91-92
Reserves; see Bank reserves
Russian inflation, 14

Scarcity of money, 6, 16-17
Schwartz, Anna J., 64n
Stabilization policy, 97-99
Stagflation, 55-59, 96

Tax rebates, 26, 34-35
Taxation, 34, 46
Time deposits, 49, 92
Transitional fluctuations, 47, 97
Treasury, United States, 88-90

Unemployment
    money growth and, 94-97, 105-106
    in United States, 44

Vault cash, 90
Velocity of money, 18-21, 49, 51-52

Wage contracts, 29, 52, 62
Wages, 48-50
War
    effect on prices, 8
    financing of, 107, 109
    money and prices during, 8, 35-36,
        46, 59, 107
Wholesale Price Index in United
    States, 7